A Very Altered Version of a Creat

In the spirit of recognizing that content presented herein is meant to be a jumping off point for inspiring readers to do more to grow their businesses, here's what can be done with the content inside:

- *You are free to share, copy and redistribute the material in any medium or format.*
- *You are free to adapt, remix, transform, and build upon the material for any purpose, even commercially.*

If you are able to understand these rather generous license terms, then I as licensor freely grant you the license to do with this content what your understanding permits.

Here are more terms of the license if you have read this far:

You should consider it appropriate to give the author credit. You may do so in any reasonable manner and the Author is likely to appreciate it – a lot actually.

But please, let's recognize that your usage should not in any way suggest that the Author endorses you or your use of said content. And if you choose to just reuse any content without giving appropriate credit, the circle will come back and bite you in the arse.

You may not apply legal terms or technological measures that legally restrict others from doing anything the license permits.

Some Legal Notices That Must Also Be Mentioned:

You do not have to comply with the license for elements of the material in the public domain or where your use is permitted by an applicable exception or limitation.

No warranties are given or implied.

The license may not give you all of the permissions necessary for your intended use. For example, other rights such as publicity, privacy, or moral rights may limit how you use the material.

To Sari, Lena, Rebecca, Raquel and Gideon
Thanks for pushing me to come home for dinner.

I Need More Clients

DIGITAL MARKETING STRATEGIES THAT CAN GROW YOUR BUSINESS

JASON CIMENT | WWW.GETVISIBLE.COM

Table of *Contents*

Chapter 1: Introduction

Hello Professional Services Provider

If you are like me, you want to grow your business.

Whether you are a lawyer, an accountant, a consultant, or any other type of professional services provider, your goals are still the same:

- **Bring in more leads who turn into clients; and**
- **Who can pay their bills (mostly on time); and**
- **Put more money in your [virtual] bank account**.

Growing one's business is supposed to be a pretty simple formula if you ask the sales gurus like Jay Abraham or Chet Holmes.

Just get in front of customers who can afford or at least find a way to finance or pay for the products and/or services you want to sell to them.

Pretty simple right?

Marketing gurus often describe this business success formula more visually by talking about finding pools of hungry fish where you can simply throw in some attractive bait and wait for the fish to bite.

The fish can't help but chomp down on the alluring and captivating bait.

And wallah, you have new customers.

But seriously, if growing one's business were as easy as fishing, we wouldn't need books and videos to teach us how to do it.

We would all just watch the 1992 film ("A River Runs Through It") with Robert Redford and be expert fly-fishermen inside of 3 hours.

So what motivated me to write this guide?

> **I began to write this book for two reasons:**
>
> 1. It's not so easy to grow one's business regardless of what you believe in or hope for.
> 2. It's even harder to grow a sustainable business when times are tough and you are already overworked.

One of the frustrations in a service oriented business is wasting time with prospects that are never going to turn into clients - either because they won't pay what you want to charge or they are committed to work with someone else and they are just using you as a sounding board.

The business books that teach sales tactics advise readers to qualify customers before going down the rabbit hole of nurturing and selling them and products or services.

Rather than me talking about the important of qualifying prospects, let's actually do a qualifying test now and see if you are a good prospect to read this book and if you should actually bother reading the rest of what is written below.

Is This Book Worth Reading?

1. Do you feel that your own business is primarily referral based?
2. Do you feel that most new clients come from existing clients?
3. Do your clients come from your social or business relationships?
4. Do you feel that your type of client base does not use the Web to find people like you for their needs (and that they want to be referred to a service provider)?

If you answered yes to these above questions and you think that there are no other extremely productive ways to find clients, then you might want to put this book down and use it as a coaster on your desk.

Before tossing away the book though, let me share a story that recently happened to a client of ours in Los Angeles.

The $650/hr Lawyer Who Thought Web Marketing Was A Waste

If, after reading this story, you want something like this to happen for your business, then keep reading. If you think that this story cannot be replicated, then seriously stop reading this book and give it away.

My client is a lawyer who at this stage of his career is a sort of senior statesman in his field of law. When we first met, he had owned a really high value domain name that at the time we met was being completely underutilized. It was simply not being promoted at all.

"But My Prospects Don't Search Online.
My Practice is Referral-Based."

What is important is to know that his billing rate was $650 an hour and for a number of years he had been convinced that his type of clients did not go online to find lawyers in his area of law.

His decades of personal experience in obtaining new clients from referrals was a <u>self-fulfilling prophecy</u> in the sense that he never advertised online or promoted his website anywhere online to attract new clients.

Since he didn't market his website, it was sort of obvious to any outsider that he would not get business from the website.

But it was not obvious to him.

This is why people tell lawyers not to represent themselves in lawsuits.

When you are too close to something ... *you can fill in the rest*.

Instead of exploring how his prospective clients were actually finding him, he just continued year after year assuming that he was "never" going to get new clients - or even referrals - from his website.

Better Looking Websites Convert More Prospects

The attorney really did want a new website to enhance his digital reputation, because he knew a better looking and more efficiently organized website would at least help him convert more people that were referred to him.

> ❖ *We always say to clients that (from a reputation perspective), their websites should look as expensive and professional as their highly valued billing rates.*

Our client was totally sold on this idea of upgrading the look and feel of his website to correlate with his leadership role in his area of law.

But he was never sold on the idea that a newly optimized website would make a difference in terms of attracting new clients from search engine listings.

His lack of enthusiasm just produced months of unnecessary delays.

After agreeing to have us redesign and rebuild his website, this high-powered lawyer consistently delayed the completion of the site (due to other priorities) and was clearly not motivated to let us finish his website in our typically streamlined manner.

Let me tell you what happened to my very smart lawyer client.

How We Turned a Brochure Site Into an Explosive Lead Generator

- We completed the design and built him a site in WordPress.
- We embedded optimizations into the coding for SEO purposes.
- We installed WordPress plugins that made the site even more attractive to Google's search engine spiders.
- We helped guide him as he wrote more compelling web copy on the site to highlight his relevant legal services.

- We worked with him to improve the keyword effectiveness of his "meta" descriptions and web page titles.
- We added keyword rich headlines to each page (i.e. H1 and H2 and H3 tags) to add content relevancy to each page.
- We helped him republish dozens of highly informative articles he had posted over the years that Google was not adequately ranking.

So what do you think happened to his reputation after the site launch?

In 6 Months Clients Were Coming Out Of The Ductwork

The attorney's self-fulfilling fantasy of just using his website as a brochure, quite simply, fell apart.

People started visiting his site in numbers he never anticipated - and those people were not just browsing his site needlessly. They were filling out leads forms and calling his very clear phone number.

Within six months of relaunching his new website, his lead volume skyrocketed and shattered all his expectations. I mean this seriously.

For the purposes of privacy, I can't give you an exact number or tell you what city or state he is located in. It's really not necessary.

Things to Remember From This Section

1. If you are a lawyer or any type of service provider, you have an obligation to investigate how people find firms like YOURS in the industry in which you practice.

2. Find 3 competitors of yours who have strong looking websites online. Go to www.SEMRush.com and type in their URLs (one search at a time) into the tool and see the results. You can instantly see keyword phrases each site is ranking for in Google AND you can see if they are buying PPC ads for different phrases as well.

3. Take the same 3 competitor URLs and let's do an investigation in the Google Adwords keyword tool to see what these sites are doing in Google.

   Go to www.Google.com/Adwords (you may have to sign up for an account, and don't worry it's free) and go to the Keyword Planner (under Tools). Just type in the URL and see what keywords Google attributes to each site.

4. Now that you have been able to see a list of keyword phrases that may be relevant to your service business, here is the last step. Go back to the Keyword Planner tool (while you are logged in to your Google account) and type in some of the phrases and see two things:
   - How many searches per month are happening per phrase?
   - How much people are bidding for each click per phrase?

5. Take our quiz.
   - If you are not optimizing your website to its maximum lead-generation potential, you will never know how many possible clients you are losing per year.
   - Don't fall into the dangerous trap of thinking, "But my practice has always been referral-based. *Therefore, my clients couldn't be searching for me on the internet."*
   - Relationship building and networking are great, so is a 100% optimized website. See the Appendix for great articles on networking and other business development tactics.

If you feel that your business is only going to grow from your personal relationships, then toss this book into a recycle bin or give it away to someone you know that needs more help growing their business.

The Appendix is going to include some great articles on networking and other business development tactics.

If you are ready to keep reading, then let's take the plunge and start growing your lead pipeline to find you more clients.

Chapter 2: Introducing "P6", The 6 Part Biz Dev Recipe

The 6 P's of Sustainable Business Growth

You may be asking how you can learn to create and implement your own system to grow your professional services business. There are different kinds of layers to peel away when coming up with a focused strategy to grow your business online.

Introducing Your First Biz Dev Recipe: P6

P6 is the underlying philosophy that contributes to an ongoing, profitable and sustainable business. P6 is essentially a recipe that includes SIX (6) high-level ingredients:

1. **PACKAGE** a clear and compelling offer
2. **PRESENT** this offer again and again
3. To different groups of targeted **PEOPLE**
4. That **PERCEIVE** they need what you are offering
5. Who **PREFER** you over your competitors
6. And they can **PAY** for what they buy from you

Solar Powered Online Lead Generation - Even In The Dark

I am going to break things down into bite-size pieces and help you implement a step-by-step online lead generation strategy that will enable YOUR business to survive and thrive in good times and in bad ones too. My goals therefore in this book are to share long-lasting ideas and lessons and a framework of tasks that can help you use the Internet to not only grow your business now but keep it growing year after year.

Now if you are thinking that this recipe sounds simplistic, you should know that just because something sounds easy does not really mean that it is easy to achieve. And that is why this book can be helpful.

Let's break this six-part recipe down a bit though to understand how complex it really is and how its ingredients can be reformulated into something you can really bite into and use for your own business goals.

2.1 Package & Present: What People Miss

Let's start with the first two ingredients:

- Packaging your offer, and
- Presenting it in front of more and more people again and again

What these ingredients suggest is more subtle than you think because people tend to read them at face value and miss out on the nuances.

For a transactional business, for ongoing success you need to know that there is a market ready to both buy what you are selling and pay the price you are asking. Whether the market exists or you create it, you need ready and willing buyers - whether it's a product or a service.

Let's start with the offer. Whether it's a service or a product, your offer should ideally follow a pattern where it is:

- *defined,*
- *refined,*
- *precise, and*
- *compelling*

Ask 2 questions. What problem are you solving? Who are you solving it for? Use a telescope to look forward to the end result and then work backwards to develop your communication and engagement strategy.

You can "sex up" your messaging with "neuro-linguistic programming" (e.g. mind tricks that sort of hypnotize the reader to take certain actions) and savvy marketing copy, but plainly and simply, there has to be a point where the mechanics of your value propositions must be conveyed to visitors so that "they understand what you are offering" clearly and quickly.

Know How To Package Your "Offer"

In a certain sense, you want to first design the whole tapestry of what you can do and then thread the needle throughout your design to take care of the details.

The precursor to "packaging your offer" is to first <u>know as much as you can</u> about what is being offered in the marketplace of competitors.

If you want to frame your service offerings in such a way that you look appealing and stand out from other providers of similar services, you need to dig much deeper than you might expect to really understand what is you can do for clients that makes you seem more desirable than other providers.

Here's an example of digging deeper.

If you are a lawyer, then your gut response at a networking event is to describe yourself as a person (or a firm) that offers legal services. "Hey, what do you do? Oh, I'm a lawyer." It's hard to be more irresistible than this typical response, right?

If you were really interested in making a connection to the person who asked what you do, at the very least you would go into more details in terms of the type of law you practice and the different practice areas your firm covers.

Look at it this way. It's just not very sexy to say "I'm a bankruptcy attorney" when you can say "I specialize in bankruptcy law for businesses who need a Chapter 13 expert."

The act of "packaging your offer" is merely a way of saying you need to be more expressive and find a way to break through the white noise so you can gain attention to YOUR [hopefully] unique brand.

What you want to convey with your brand is this expectation of EXCELLENCE - which is not just about the output on your site. It's also about the input. What are you doing to be excellent? What are you reading? What are you eating? What are you doing to produce a celebration of excellence that finds its way into your core values?

Let's Talk About an Employment Lawyer

As a brief example, let's take an employment attorney and highlight a few different ways this attorney can describe his or her service offerings:

- A simple version of an offer is "I practice employment law."
- A more complex version of this offer is "I practice employment law and represent employers."
- Going deeper … "I represent companies and businesses in the aerospace industry who need a law firm that specializes in employment law."

In all three of these cases, if a prospect is looking at your law firm website to learn more about what you do, there can be a link in the navigation menu (e.g. that bar of links across the top of a web page) called LEGAL SERVICES than can direct the visitor to an internal section of the website that describes your firm's "practice areas."

This practice areas section can include one page that lists all the different subsets of employment law. As well, if you have spent the time to invest in more verbose pages, this section can be enhanced by including different web pages for each sub-specialty within your larger arena of employment law.

Since we have been talking about an employer side law firm, here are examples of how you could extend your practice areas section:

- Employee handbooks.
- Sexual harassment training.
- Rules about breaks and meal plans.

How does all this lead into the goal of packaging the offer?

To start with, the "packaging" ecosystem also describes the process of highlighting your offer in a way that commands attention of the viewer.

Let's try this analogy by borrowing some marketing techniques from the automobile industry.

Just because cars get you from here to there, does not mean all cars are equal. Nor does it mean that people perceive cars to be the same.

Two effective ways manufacturers distinguish their cars are by:

- Designing cars with varied features and different price tags
- Building showrooms and promotional campaigns that set their cars apart from each other (and competitors' cars)

In the context of a law firm website, we can take the analogy of a car manufacturer and learn some valuable lessons.

Each of your legal practice areas is like a feature of a car.

Just like two cars can have 4 cylinder engines that perform differently, you can have two law firms both doing employment law that provide different levels of service - even within the same or similar practice areas of law.

But this distinction in terms of features is only part of the decision-making process for a consumer who buys a car or a person looking to hire an employment lawyer.

Don't Forget The "Selling" Mindset

Remember, the automotive customer needs to be "sold" before committing to make a purchase. Just because a car has certain features does not mean a purchase is forthcoming.

And this is where "packaging the offer" of the P6 Recipe can add value to our analysis.

In the same way a car company like Toyota builds a website and drives traffic to the website (and to its physical showrooms) by running commercials on TV, print ads in newspapers, video ads online and broadcast spots on radio, a law firm often has to undergo a similar step-by-step marketing process.

Toyota needs to gets it cars in front of buyers again and again because cars are not usually an impulse buy.

Toyota has to run TV ads repeatedly, build beautiful showrooms usually in highly trafficked areas, create glossy magazine displays and showcase the features of its cars online in beautiful videos merely to package the value of its cars in a way that commands attention in a busy arena.

A lawyer needs to do the same thing by starting with the building of a website and in some cases the corollary social media properties such as Facebook, Twitter and LinkedIn.

And that is just the essence of the "packaging" framework.

Let's Do a "Packaging" Review

What People Misunderstand About "Packaging" An Offer

1. People think "packaging" is just saying what YOU do instead of saying what you do for YOUR CLIENTS that produces results.
2. Prospects in a service business need to be sold again and again.
3. Packaging leads ultimately to trusting - which is something you have to earn because it's not given freely by your clients.
4. A "me too" brochure website can never compete with a "professionally intentioned" website.

Packaging is a mindset you need to embrace that says "I am going to find a way to talk to the clients I want to reach in a way THEY want to be talked to so I can get under their radar and establish a hypnotic connection that starts the process of converting each of them into a prospect and ultimately into a lead."

Since this book is primarily about growing your client funnel through online methods, your Internet presence must also package your service offerings in such a way that you look like you can not only deliver the "goods" but also outperform your competitors.

This goal does not mean that your website has to be expensive and have the latest gadgets and apps. But your website has to be presentable and that's what we are going to talk about with the 2nd ingredient of P6.

2.2 "Presenting" Is Being Sensitive To The Bounce Moment

Your site needs to be CLEAN AND INTUITIVE so that people will quickly know what you do and like what they see before they either worry about figuring out how good you are or worse, leave the site.

I think of this moment of encounter as a test of whether that visitor will decide to stay or leave (i.e. bounce). That decision moment happens fast - so fast, the person does not even realize a decision is being made.

(WIIFM) What's In It For Me?

Will your visitor stay, or bounce? The Bounce Moment occurs in the lizard part of your brain - the instinctive part of your brain that has existed and has been evolving since the creation of man. This part of your brain NEEDS TO KNOW "what this page is offering to do for me" - what marketers call the "what's in it for me" syndrome.

Winning The 6 Second War

When we create a commercial website for a client, one of our initial discussions concerns what we want to happen at that **moment of encounter** when a person first lands on any page of the website we've built. We think we have less than 6 seconds.

First-time visitors don't need to know if your web page is good or bad at this point. They just need to know what the offer is that they see - and on some primal level "is it safe to even be on this page."

There is a lot of crossover between packaging and presenting an offer because once you have figured out what you want your clients want to hear (in regards to what services you offer), you have to find ways to get this message across in a way that it will be received.

And because of the "engagement moment" concept, you've got just a few seconds to sustain a connection with visitors to your website.

If you are an employment attorney, then your "engagement moment" has to convey quite simply the idea that you do employment law - and explain a little bit what that means in plain enough terms that people can quickly grasp the gist of what you do before they start the process of trusting you and digging deeper to first get to know you.

Getting back to our example, at this moment of encounter stage, your law firm website could also highlight that you represent the employers and NOT employees.

Beware of TMI Pitfalls

Just be careful not to distract visitors with too much info at this initial stage. Even trying to convey the message that you have been doing this for 25 years could sometimes be TMI (too many ingredients).

What Most People Misunderstand About Presenting Online

1. Timing is critical. You can't throw a plate of spaghetti at someone and expect them to find the one noodle that meets their needs. Your messaging needs to come in stages so that you can coax people step by step through your brand value ecosystem.
2. It's not necessarily what you say, but how you say it that matters even more.
3. This is why images and videos are so powerful because they can transform any message into something more "presentable."

Think of your website as a very shiny container that has to attract and keep someone's attention in such a way that your value propositions (i.e. your services) can be conveyed before someone leaves the site.

Who are these people we have to present our offers to?

We can more formally address audience targeting by revisiting our P6 recipe and looking at the 3rd ingredient which is PEOPLE.

This question is a great segue to something my SEO (search engine optimization) team internally describes as AUDIENCE SEGMENTATION.

This is the process of looking at your total audience of potential customers and clients and breaking this audience up into multiple smaller, like-minded audiences. There is a strict logic to this mindset.

Your business can't be <u>everything to *everyone*</u>.

But your business can be <u>everything to *someone*</u>.

The more you can find people who think you are "their everything", the more business you should be able to bring in - again and again.

2.3 Avoid Mass Exposure. Get In Front of the "Right People"

Let's put this into concrete terms with an example in a totally different industry so that we don't get overwhelmed with law firm examples.

This Vegan restaurant (let's use "Real Food Daily" since it's near where I live in Los Angeles) has a greater chance to increase its revenue base if it can consistently appeal individually to each of the four different types of patrons it can please.

A Vegan restaurant often has various types of customers.

1. People who are lactose intolerant.
2. People who avoid animal products.
3. People who eat it periodically (healthier lifestyle).
4. People who love eating fake meat with fake cheese on fake bread – nothing wrong with that of course.

And it's a viciously successful cycle because the more that patrons feel that the restaurant is catering to their needs, the more successful Real Food Daily will be in attracting these customers time and time again.

Wouldn't this type of audience targeting approach produce a more positive outcome for your business if you could reach multiple groups of like-minded clients?

Real Food Daily has to get into the mindset of these multiple segments of potential patrons. It then has to come up with a strategy get its brand in front of these groups of customers to drive them into the restaurant.

Since this book is really focused on marketing a business online let's keep going with this restaurant example and talk about what Real Food Daily should be doing with its www.RealFood.com website.

Clearly it needs to reach out to more customers online and get its menu in front of them - and if not the menu, at least the name of the restaurant and its location and the fact that it is a Vegan non-dairy, non-meat, food eatery.

Depeche Mode Didn't Get It Right. People Are Not Just People

Real Food Daily needs to connect intimately to each customer base with a messaging strategy that is appealing to that group's needs and tastes.

One of the key approaches to reaching each group is to do some research to find out where each of these groups of potential patrons aggregate and gather online - not necessarily because they are looking for a vegan restaurant - but simply to see if there are places online that Real Food can promote itself and be noticed by them.

Real Food Daily has to figure out where these 4 segments of potential customers hang out online and then find a way to get in front of them - and for a cost that makes profitable sense.

It Might Be Time to Do a Spock Mind Meld

Consider that identifying and reaching out to your different audience segments may involve two sides of the same coin.

- First, get into the minds of your different clients to figure out how to categorize these disparate groups of people into multiple audience segments that share something in common.
- Then you have to analyze each of the audience segments and figure out their browsing habits to see where they go online to find companies like yours and then get in front of them.

Once you have figured these 2 things out, you simply have to initiate moments of introduction which will enable you to ...

- Drive these segments of targeted people to your website,
- Introduce them to your brand identity, and
- Pitch them (showcase your offers and your intrinsic value).

By now maybe it's clearer that getting your offer in front of people incorporates many integrated core goals.

1. Know your offer and make it clear to your leads/customers.
2. This is wrapped in something we call "packaging your offer".
3. Figure out the groups (e.g. segments) of customers to reach.
4. Find out where these customers can be reached online.
5. Find an economic way to get in front of them again and again.

Action Item for You:

Write down things you do for clients; and, the types of services you offer.

- *Try to categorize your services so it's not just a big laundry list.*
- *Then write down some positioning statements that are like soundbites that describe what you do.*
- *Write short versions and long versions.*

Now put this aside as we continue.

Let's discuss the 4th ingredient of our P6 success recipe - namely how customers perceive your offer in terms of their own needs.

2.4 Catering to Audience "Perceptions"

Instead of talking about Real Food Daily, let's go back and discuss the employment attorney scenario.

In that example, there are two major targeted audience segments the employment lawyer can immediately identify at the beginning of an audience segmentation analysis review.

1. The Employees who get terminated (or need protection while employed)
2. The Employers who hire and fire people they employ.

Often employment attorneys will represent one of these two segments of clients and gain a reputation as an Employer side or Employee side law firm.

This is an important distinction because how clients think of your services is part of their decision making process when they hire you.

And if they think you sit on both sides of the fence, that reputation may not be as compelling to a person who just got fired that wants a lawyer who specializes in suing companies for wrongful termination.

There's No Right or Wrong Answer Here.

What's important for you as the lawyer to think about is what could be lurking in your client's mind during the decision making process of which lawyer to hire.

So if you do straddle the fence and you want to win more business:

*   Then you can play it up in your marketing copy by saying we know what employers are thinking because we also represent employers, and/or
*   You can reverse it as well if you are pitching an employer as a client and say "we know what employees are thinking about ..."

Can we learn anything valuable from knowing that employment lawyers have multiple sets of client types?

If your law firm represents people in the food services industry like waiters and cooks, C-level executives of restaurant chains, then you can boast about your industry expertise and be perceived as a market leader representing the full range of employees.

More Can Be Better With Your Content

The more granular you can be in your web copy (through blog postings for example) about your industry experience, the more chances you will have to both drive more leads (from search rankings) and close those leads due to your perceived industry authority. This of course assumes you have a good website too.

This is pretty serious stuff when it comes to marketing and establishing the authority of your "brand identity" online.

If you have messaging on your site that talks about providing legal services to restaurants, food distributors, farms, and other types of companies along the food distribution chain, it gives your firm the air of superiority over other lawyers who might be competing for similar clients but don't have as much to say to back up their credibility.

With smart web copy, you can expand your perception from servicing just restaurants to the entire food industry. Your content messaging strategy should include videos, client testimonials and digital media.

When we review this 4th PERCEPTION ingredient of the P6 success formula which suggests that your customers must believe that they **need or want** what you have to offer, we have a lot to talk about.

Are You Familiar with the Cult of Provisors?

I belong to a networking organization called Provisors (www.Provisors.com) where professional service providers gather at least once a month to facilitate introductions for each other's businesses.

The organization has a wonderful mantra for growing a referral based business.

Know – Like – Trust – Refer

In the Provisors world, I meet lawyers, CPAs, bankers, consultants, insurance brokers, IT companies and a host of other providers who build their entire book of business by giving and receiving referrals.

If you break down their mantra into its working components, it makes a lot of sense even in our digital marketing conversation.

Want to Manipulate Visitor Perceptions?

I'll use a story to illustrate this idea and walk you through many of the component ideas to think about as you execute a P6 campaign.

- Jim, a manager of a restaurant chain in Louisville, Kentucky, has been fired.

- He uses Google to research if other people have been terminated in similar circumstances (or even terminated by the same company).
- He types in different sorts of keyword phrases such as "manager of Burger King fired for bad reason" in Google and Bing.

- In the search results (and the PPC ads) he finds listings directing him to different websites with relevant content inside blog posts, case studies and even videos on YouTube.

- Jim starts reading these stories and watching these videos (did you know in certain cases 70% of people would rather watch a video than read something).

- Jim starts to feel empowered as he gets more educated about what it means to be fired and what he could possibly do about getting compensated for it (or getting his job back).

Jim see this very long-winded website from an employment law firm (e.g. www.KentuckyRestaurantLawyers.com) that talks about its history of successes in suing restaurants that wrongfully terminate employees.

A person like Jim - who does not have a personal connection to a lawyer (let alone an employment lawyer) - is likely to take that very encouraging step (but an easy step if the website is designed well) and reach out through the site to ask for more information.

- Jim might call the number (that is supposed to be discernable on all pages of the website),

- Fill out a form to explain his issue, or

- Drop a message via a social channel like Twitter or Facebook.

This is not a wildly fantastical scenario. This is one of the very effective and consistent ways that website marketing or digital branding efforts bring businesses new clients and new customers.

I go deeper, I want to share with you that I have attempted to sneak something subtle into this case study by the way.

If you look at the name of the law firm's website above, it had a bit of neuro-linguistic programming built in.

The URL contained three discrete messages sandwiched into the domain name that were designed to make an impact on Jim (and you) subconsciously and reinforce the lizard brain response:

- Kentucky
- Restaurant
- Lawyers

The first subtle message is the mentioning of [the State of] Kentucky.

The name of the State in the URL (i.e. domain name) planted the seed in Jim's mind that the firm has a geographic relevance to him because of that fact that he was working in Louisville and the website is connected to Kentucky.

If Jim were able during his investigation to later feel that this firm could relate to his situation, the first subtle message that has already been implanted (like a hypnotic suggestion) is that the firm has some tangible connection to Kentucky.

I will elaborate on this point a little more for the sake of clarity.

At the preliminary lizard stage when Jim has just encountered this website, Jim does not even consciously know that it's a law firm because he's only seen the word Kentucky.

But that's fine, because there are multiple barriers to win Jim's trust that the law firm will have to overcome as Jim continues to see if this website is a good fit for him.

We will discuss more about these barriers as we continue.

The second subtle message I snuck into the domain is the word "Restaurant."

Again, Jim's lizard brain is seeing in the word "restaurant", another word that has a tangible connection to his current job and profession.

The building blocks are starting to pile up in Jim's mind that he has stumbled onto someone or some company that might have something relevant to offer him because he worked in the food business in Kentucky.

Finally, he sees the word "lawyers" - again in the domain name.

And now the first two implanted messages start to make a lot more sense to his lizard brain.

And when all three messages get combined, the journey of the digital brand value starts moving from Jim's subconscious mind to his conscious mind where his decision making process can be manipulated.

Jim has found a law firm that represents people who may have been fired like him - and this firm is located specifically in the place where he works (or worked at least until recently) and provides legal services in the area of business he works in.

Let's return to our PERCEPTION ingredient:

Targeting audience segments that have a perception they need whatever it is you are offering to them.

- We described how a firm wrote articles, blog posts, and case studies and made videos that described people who got wrongfully terminated and the legal services they needed.
- We talked about how this Kentucky law firm did these things to attract employees who have been terminated like Jim.

It's worth mentioning that this domain name has a potential deficiency because the word "restaurant" can also be restricting.

- o If Jim were a manager of a food processor, he might not be so inclined to believe that this firm can help him.
- o He might feel this firm is too focused on restaurants.
- o Then it would up to the firm's website to direct him to a page to learn about the firm's work with other companies in the food business chain.

A better domain might be www.KentuckyFoodLegalGroup.com if the firm wanted to be perceived as being an authority with industry relevance to more companies in the food business arena.

Let's talk as well about companies and businesses that EMPLOY people who work in the food chain and how they also need legal services. How would such a law firm in Kentucky attract these types of clients?

The first thing is identifying what these EMPLOYERS need from a law firm. *(This should remind you of our discussion on packaging your offer.)*

If businesses are hiring and firing employees, they need:

- • Legal documents like employment and termination agreements
- • Employment handbooks (that govern ongoing operations)
- • Help with a whole host of other regulatory requirements from city, state and Federal authorities

If the firm wants to attract attention from employers then its blogs, videos, and case studies would have to be nuanced to talk about things such as employment and termination agreements. A great example of a lawyer that has put this branding strategy into practice is George Salmas at www.TheFoodLawyers.com.

It's about time to move full force onto the 5th ingredient (PREFER) which is where you start convincing people that you are BETTER than other lawyers.

Winning the Vendor Preference Game

We can still spend a little bit more time on tactics you can execute on your website and how these items can impact what we should think of going forward as your digital brand identity.

Note that we have to take things a level deeper here.

This is because for every savvy lawyer there are 10 other savvy lawyers who also have good domain names and good web copy - and may have read this book (or others like it).

So the question is: "how do you get a leg up for your services business when there is serious competition in your space for marketing your type of firm online?"

<u>Here are two subtle things you can do</u> that will give you a better chance of connecting your professional services to the people and companies that need them or will make referrals to someone else.

1. **Give some of your individual services a brand name.**
2. **Get a vanity phone number that makes an impact.**

The idea behind a brand name is to give people the impression of two things: (1) that this is not your first time to the dance; and (2) that you have created a process around your service.

Let me explain this further.

People naturally are attracted to systems that suggest success. They don't want to be guinea pigs.

They want to know that you have a plan which you have done before and that you can repeat again for them - even if it has to be customized and personalized for their situation.

Divers have a system they call "plan the dive, dive the plan" which reinforces itself every time they dive.

Airplane pilots have a very cumbersome checklist because one item missed can mean a plane crash.

How to put these two subtle ideas into practice:

Take an ordinary employment handbook you have used for years. Start calling it "The Bulletproof Restaurant Employment Handbook."

All of a sudden, the boring handbook has become bulletproof and it's focused on restaurants.

What is one of the employer's biggest fears with employees? Getting sued by an employee. *Often employees can sue just to threaten an employer as a sort of blackmail – especially in employee friendly states like California.*

And, when an employer sees a law firm offering a bulletproof handbook, don't you think that is going to make a huge impression and shock them out of their trance of wanting to ignore the information about your employee handbook just like they ignore everyone else's handbook description too?

And like the weightlifter hitting that 16th repetition, or the guys from Spinal Tap hitting 11 on the volume dial, you can turn it up a notch with the branding strategy above.

Put a Trademark symbol ™ after the handbook name to give it that official stamp that says you didn't just name your process (that protects employers from angry and deceitful employees), you protected your process too.

And if you want, you can even make an acronym out of the name of the handbook. I came up with H.E.R.B. by jumbling the letters around.

I am definitely not suggesting that this is a great acronym but it is still better than nothing and it can make some subtle impact to the reader.

All these little subtleties are building blocks to be used in the game of connecting more intimately with your target audiences.

Remember, the Know-Like-Trust-Refer mantra?

Whatever you can do to create this 4-step "flow", this "Exchange," just do it.

The more the pieces add up into a complete picture that makes some kind of sense (to the lizard and the rest of the brain) – even if there are still some missing puzzle pieces – the more likely it will be that you convert them and win their business.

As you continue reading, keep this formula in mind because it's just another way of saying you should look for ways to use your website to create the appearance of a relationship of trust because this fosters more business transactions.

Are You Geared for Referrals?

Let's review where we are in this law firm example before we get to the 5th ingredient of our P6 success formula.

1. Your firm offers employment law services (mostly in Kentucky).
2. Your firm specializes in representing employers - i.e. the businesses that need an employment law firm.
3. You have done an audience segmentation analysis and learned that there are specific industries to target (e.g. food, environmental testing, waste management) in your geographic reach in Kentucky that have a big demand for your legal services.
4. You have created landing pages for each of these audience segments describing some of the services you can offer that are contextualized to each reader.
5. You have created specialized content in the form of blogs, articles and/or videos to address each audience segment. We will address this in more detail later on in this book.

If we look at www.KentuckyFoodLegalGroup.com, we can use the same domain name and change the messaging to target Employers instead of Employees and still get many benefits.

- Companies in the food industry would see Kentucky in the domain and feel there is a geographic trust factor they can mark off on their internal checklist.
- Then they would see the word "food" in the domain and get another reason to mark their checklist with a checkmark for industry relevance.
- And finally, they would see the word "Legal Group" in the domain name and see that this site is from a law firm.

2.5 Be Preferred & Win The "Would You Rather" Game

The 5th ingredient says: "Do things that inspire trust" so that you can convince people to PREFER you over alternative choices.

When people reach a web page there is a 3-fold challenge that exists in order to win their trust and keep them from leaving. In the visitor's mind, there are 3 roadblocks (like a toll-gate) with security guards who are instructed to tell the visitor to leave the site unless 3 needs are satisfied:

1. The site is clear about what it is about.
2. The site is clear about who is being addressed.
3. The site is clear about why it should be trusted.

If you have a web page and you want your digital branding message to grab your visitor's attention and bypass the security guards, you must address these 3 items.

Every Website Has 3 Trapdoors To Avoid

In this case study, we are going to talk about a different type of person who works for a company that would be a typical business client for our example law firm.

Here's how the 3 gates idea works for this employment law firm website (where the URL does not even hint to the firm's specific specialty in food law):

1. Sally reaches the www.KentuckyEmploymentLawyers.com site.
   - Her lizard brain instantly figures out the firm offers employment law services.
   - And she needs a new employee handbook.
   - So she knows she is in the right place in terms of what the site does.

2. Sally is the head of HR for a candy company in Kentucky. Sally feels she is even more in the right place because the firm is has offices in Kentucky. She can check this item off the list and start to raise the 2nd gate.

3. There are still 4 things Sally doesn't yet know:
   - What type of employment law practice this is;
   - Does it represent employees or employers; and,
   - What industry specialties exist (like food).
   - Is the firm [really] good? Can its partners be trusted?

The 3rd item on our list (really two items) which I think of as the trust phase is sometimes the toughest to overcome. Inspiring trust takes on many forms in the digital brand messaging game.

There are many ways to INSPIRE TRUST and most of them are pretty much under the radar in a sense but become quite visible in a negative way if you don't adhere to these rules.

Naturally this Kentucky law firm wants Sally's security guard to lift that 3rd gate so she can stay on the site and request more information (by filling out a lead form and initiating the whole lead nurturing process).

Here are just a few examples of things this Kentucky law firm can do on its website to inspire trust (and we'll dig deeper later on):

- Avoid typos on the website.
- Make sure all the links work (do 404 testing monthly)
- Showcase industry awards
- Highlight years of experience and/or in specific industries
- Signup for at least one social media account like Facebook, Twitter or LinkedIn and put the links on your website.
- Match the visual imagery and branding of your website inside your social media pages. Meaning its Facebook page should appear visually related to its website.
- If your partners are a selling point, then have rich Team Profiles with good photos and strong web copy that is more than just a few boring sentences or me too type paragraphs.
- Publish to its blog at least 2x per month to show the Firm is current with relevant legal trends, settlements and cases.
- Unless the blog is totally just fun in which case that can be a powerful "trust" strategy too.
- Have a fresh, compelling looking website that is not more than two years out of date in terms of styling.
- Promote a YouTube video which presents something more compelling than just text and images on a web page.
- Display testimonials and references from clients or other authorities that would matter to each audience segment.
- Write case studies (and drop names) that people will recognize.
- Don't use photos from image libraries that are inappropriate.
- Make it easy and intuitive to navigate the website.
- Display contact info really clearly on every page.
- If physical location matters, display the address on all pages.

To get people to trust that you can deliver the goods ([or services], you have to invest in goodwill and create an online identity that supports your brand.

- o Present web site visitors with an engaging story
- o Present your firm as competent, timely, and endorsed.
- o Add likeability factors that tell visitors that you are both really good at what you do and that people agree with this and like working with you.
- o Don't be a jerk - unless being a jerk is something you think people want.
- o Be cool. Be fun. Be desirable. Be easy.

2.6 Are You Still Holding Your Engagement Ring?

Let's uncover the last and most important P in our recipe - Payment.

P6 Recipe — Package — Present — People — Perceive — Prefer — Pay

Getting in front of those targeted groups of people that can actually <u>PAY for what you are offering</u>.

Think of it this way. It's nice to go to the dance but not if you leave the party without a date. It's great to date seriously, but greater to marry.

Business school books are filled with stories of companies with great ideas that people said they wanted but weren't prepared to pay for.

Sometimes like the Newton, your product might be ready before its time and the "need" is not yet there and you can't force it either.

Other times the cost is simply too much of a barrier to entry to enable your company to "take off" and be a success.

As much as we've been discussing "audience segmentation" and "offer differentiation", you've got to qualify customers.

Even obvious things need to be stated and restated once in a while.

1. Ask tough questions up front. Don't waste resources on people that are not likely to be good clients (or good lead sources).
2. Use the contact form on your website to give people choices where they can almost self-select themselves out of your orbit.
   a. If you say choose a service from a list of services, if the list does not include the service they want, they will abandon the form.
3. If you put a price range down and start at $5,000 for example, then if they have a $2,000 budget, they won't bother you.
4. Of course this has risk too because a $2,000 client can often be upsold into the $5,000 level. And this is a similar risk by listing a limited range of services where people may feel you don't offer the service they think they need.

Here's a quick review of the GETTING MORE CLIENTS system:

- **You have to design and build a web presence identity**
  - **Website and/or social media properties**
- **That connects with your audience segments, and**
- **Gets them to learn about you (know),**
- **Gets them to like and trust your experience & endorsements,**
- **So that they will either:**
  - **Do business with you, or**
  - **Make a referral to someone else who will work with you**

Time for a Homework Assignment.

Pull out the notebook with your list of services (i.e. offers)

- Make a list of 3 competitor websites and visit their sites.
- Write down the services they are offering
- Write down the types of clients they are targeting.
- List keyword phrases and topics they are using that people would be typing into Google as a relevant search query.
- Print out pages from these sites that grab your interest.
- Mark up the areas of the web pages that inspire trust. (Refer to the list of trust factors mentioned previously).
- Review a few pages from your own site in light of what you've learned so far. Make notes about changes you might want to address. Don't do them yet because there are more tactics coming that you'll need to consider first.
- Write down your own list of audience segments to see how many niches you can identify that would be good candidates for individualized landing pages.
- Go through your own offers (e.g. practice areas) and break them down into discrete pieces with more detailed explanations.
- Look through your digital media inventory to see if you can find images and photos and videos to inject into your website and social media properties.

It's time to dig into some details and leave this section and move onto the next segment of the book where we can get more recipes for getting more clients.

Pull Out Your Action Workbook Again

We suggest revisiting at least 3-5 websites of those strong competitors where you can look again for the following items:

- How are they designed?
- Are they dated or current?
- Do they list or write about their clients' issues?
- Can you make a list of common themes mentioned in each site?
- Are there types of images being used that seem to resonate with you?
- Are there testimonials from clients that give you ideas?
- Are keyword phrases appearing over and over (write them down)?
- Are there blogs that talk about industry challenges?
- Signup for newsletters to see what they are sending to their list.
- Are competitors advertising "solutions" (branded or otherwise)?

Do competitors address specific needs that are relevant to your strengths?

Chapter 3: Getting Into the Client Mindset

"Convince" Relevant People to Trust You

As we've already uncovered, if you want to be attractive and appealing to people that visit your website, you've learned about a 6 step technique that will help you convert visitors into leads and clients.

I think that one of the underlying concepts to the P6 recipe is that on an emotional level, your website has to CONVINCE VISITORS that you are LISTENING to them and can RELATE to their situation and to their needs.

Once they become convinced of these things and that you care, the hurdle of getting them to believe you can help is much lower.

Start a Client "Needs" Investigation

Start "speaking to them" in a way that bypasses their internal safety guards. You have to get beyond the typical white noise most people experience when visiting a new site.

When we talked about packaging our offer to specific audiences and the need to know more about your clients as part of the audience segmentation analysis process, what this means is you need to know:

- Your customers' pain points,
- Your customers' needs, and
- Your customers' requirements in a solution.

This means you have to do a lot of research to understand your audience potential and how they think of the above 3 items.

You need to start accumulating as much data as you can about pain points, needs and requirements in order to have both a starting point for your audience segmentation review as well as laying the groundwork for understanding your audience love languages (look up the book if you need to).

Do an "Audience Segmentation" Analysis

Now if you done the above exercise and analyzed at least a few competitor sites, it means you should have gained some preliminary insights on how they are promoting themselves to one or more of your audience segments. Here is where its gets a little tricky.

You have to shift gears and change sides.

You have to put the competitor notes down and get into the mindset of the customers you are targeting.

How To Get Some Insights Into Keyword Phrases.

Sign up for www.Google.com/Adwords (it's free).

Go to the Keyword Planner tool and type in a competitor's website. The tool will give you a list of keyword phrases Google has tracked for this site.

Download the phrases into Excel. Start playing with your results. You will be surprised at what you find. And it's so easy to use.

Can you break up customers into groups you can target separately?

1. For Real Food Daily restaurant, we identified 4 types of patrons.
2. For the Kentucky employment law firm, we separated clients into employers and employees. We could also separate employees by:
   - Job level (i.e. Blue collar vs C-level),
   - By industry (e.g. food, manufacturing, travel), and
   - By gender (i.e. male vs female).
   - For employers we could do a segmentation analysis.
3. Can you separate clients geographically by city or neighborhood?

Could you add a series of pages into your website that address your niches separately? And can you make these pages easily accessible through the navigation system of the website?

Here's a little trick that can improve your search engine rankings for keyword phrases found on these niche pages.

When you write the individualized content for each "niche audience" page, add some links to OTHER websites that are authoritative for that niche.

So if you are writing about food processors in Chicago, link to a chamber of commerce site, link to a food industry website in Chicago, and link to a local landmark web page.

When Google sees you LINKING OUT to other website – rather than just having links coming INTO your website – that shows in a counter-intuitive way that you are more of a resource, which Google loves.

Get your notebook from your assignment above and see if you can expand on your audience segmentation analysis?

How did you do in your first audience segmentation analysis?

Please don't take this step for granted.

You cannot believe how many websites fail this very basic Marketing 101 test as they simply talk about all the things THEY CAN DO and they never talk about what the clients actually want from them.

It's so easy for a law firm to say I do this list of practice areas.

Write Keyword-Rich Niche Landing Pages

Go the extra mile and talk about your clients and the industries they are in and you'll see how much more traction you gain from referrals in addition to an increase in traffic and visibility.

Find out how each set of clients locates relevant solutions.

- Do they search online?
- Do they ask a friend
- Do they call their trusted advisors like attorneys or wealth managers?
- Do they wait to be disrupted?
- Do they go to social media sites and ask questions?
- Are there industry sites they can go to for guidance?
- Are there bloggers or influencers with big followings these clients turn to for advice?

Before we leave this section, we need to address one more very important item.

How do each of these audience segments use the Web to find solutions to their problems?

I hope it's clear that this question is just meant to focus on solutions that are relevant to you. I am sure you have your own questions like these. Keep pounding away at it.

You have just graduated to a level of understanding that suggests you recognize the necessity of investing time and resources in breaking down your market audience into different segments to target.

And knowing this then confronts you with a frustrating challenge - which is that you have to find ways to get in front of them online.

To do this, you have to learn about their browsing habits.

Find the places they will visit online and be there before your competitors when the time is right (and even before then too).

And that leads us to the next section of this book.

Chapter 4: Omni-Channel Marketing Ecosystem

Multiple Pathways To Growing Your Client Leads Funnel

When I wear my biz dev hat at **Get Visible**, my meetings tend to focus on omni-channel marketing strategies because our clients want to drive traffic from multiple sources - not just SEO. Let's jump off the ship for a moment like Jonah and get into the underbelly of tactics for driving traffic to your digital brand. (Ok. He was tossed but so what).

There are a variety of ways Molly can use the Internet to discover a restaurant like Real Food Daily:

1. Go to Google or Bing and type in a phrase like "vegan restaurant 90035" to find restaurants listed in that zip code.
2. Go to a social site like Facebook and ask her friends for a referral to a good Vegan restaurant.
3. If Molly is a foodie, she can visit a foodie site and find vegan restaurants listed in that site in an internal directory.
4. Likely because Molly wants to go to a restaurant, she may go to a site like Yelp.com and look for highly rated vegan restaurants there too.

We must first draw a distinction between two very disparate groups of customers you want to reach. Those who:

- **Know what (not who) solution they need.**
- **Need to be educated about the solution.**

Why is this distinction important?

The reason is that your market penetration strategies are going to be totally different. Let me explain.

How Do YOU Find Services And Products?

Let's talk about Molly from above, who may like vegan food and wants to experience someone else's vegan cooking tonight. She is going to go online and look for a vegan restaurant.

As you would suspect, Real Food Daily has done its market research and has some ideas of what it needs to do online to capture more attention from people like Molly who are searching online for a vegan restaurant.

Access Your Client Mindset With A "Discovery" Dump

Look at different ways Molly can do a search for a vegan restaurant on a "search engine" like Google.

When Molly goes to Google [or Bing] to find a vegan restaurant, there are a couple of realities Real Food Daily needs to be mindful of if it wants to increase its chances of getting a web page address or Facebook page or Yelp page (with a recipe, menu or name and address of the restaurant) in front of Molly on the search results page.

If you look at what I wrote I have just written above, I specifically did not say that Real Food Daily is initially only looking to get a free search engine ranking.

Instead, its overall plan is to get its restaurant listing (wherever it is listed) somewhere online directly in front of Molly - when Molly begins the process of outsourcing the preparation of a vegan meal.

This means that getting its restaurant in front of Molly can happen in more ways than just a free or paid search engine listing.

Let's start with a search engine listing since that can be the greatest source of ongoing visibility and traffic to the Real Food Daily website.

Let's remember that Molly might have many ways to type in a search query.

Understanding 2 Types of Google Searches

We also know that the more detailed her search query, the more likely she would be to go to a site that matches that query.

If Molly is looking for a great vegan pizza, she might type in "**best pizza vegan in Los Angeles**" (purposely not worded in the proper order) as her search phrase.

- If Real Food Daily has posted a photo with the caption or a file name that includes the words Vegan Pizza and the photo is geo-tagged (advanced search engine tactic) with coordinates for Los Angeles, then the photo on its website might come up high in the organic rankings.

- If Real Food Daily posted a blog entry titled "top 5 vegan pizza recipes" on its website, this page might come up high in the organic rankings too.

- If Real Food Daily created a video titled "how to make a vegan pizza" and posted it on YouTube – and geo-tagged the video to Los Angeles – then this video could also show up on the first page of search engine results.

These three examples demonstrate SEO tactics to obtain different organic rankings that could include links to the Real Food Daily website.

Each listing in the rankings is like a "brass ring" (defined here as a search result listing that links to Real Food Daily) in the form of a photo, a recipe on a food site, an actual web page on the RFD blog, or a video that might appear on the Real Food Daily site or on another site like Vimeo or YouTube.

Our analysis does not end with these three examples.

There are still many other listings on a search engine results page we can address that can help Real Food Daily attract more customers.

When Molly types in the search query looking for that great vegan restaurant, Google presents a list of web pages (called the organic listings) in its search results where usually only one of those pages is a link to the Real Food Daily website.

Other pages in the search engine listings will not be the Real Food Daily website. There will be links to other websites (like Yelp or YouTube).

But that does not preclude Real Food Daily from getting its information in front of Molly in those other organic listings.

Getting Organic Listings in Search Engines

Here are examples of how a fully loaded optimization strategy can extend Real Food Daily's digital brand reach to attract more clicks.

Here are types of highly ranking websites that could come up in the organic listings that would help Real Food Daily.

1. A Yelp page listing that includes Real Food Daily on its own web page.
2. A blogger who covers vegan eateries has created a vegan restaurant directory site.
3. A local newspaper that has a restaurant listing which includes Real Food Daily.
4. Just as an aside, Real Food Daily could also run a PPC campaign with Google Adwords and drive more traffic. I will cover more of this in the Appendix.

In these above examples, Real Food Daily can get more exposure to its site if it contacts non-competitive sites that already come up in the search results and approaches them to get its restaurant or menu or just a featured dish showcased on those sites.

The reason I say they should contact non-competitive sites is that if the other listings are restaurants that are competitive, Real Food Daily is not going to get listed or referenced on their sites - not cleanly at least.

Protecting Your Online Reputation

Considering that my wife says I have undiagnosed A.D.D. (Attention Deficit Disorder), let's explore a momentary diversion into "Reputation Management" - a segment of the search engine marketing business that is really important if you want to manage your brand footprint.

There are two sides to a Reputation Management campaign.

1. If Real Food Daily wants to be more visible, its goal is to populate as many listings as possible on the first page of search results listings for relevant searches. This is the positive side of Rep management.

2. The negative side is where someone has written a bad review of Real Food Daily and that bad review shows up in the organic listings for branded (use of Real Food Daily brand name) and even non-branded (generic keyword searches) searches. Here Real Food Daily wants to crowd out the listing that includes the bad review and "push it down" off of page one by pushing up other ranked web pages ahead of the bad review.

If you think SEO is just about ranking your website or your social media properties in the organic listings - your perspective is shortsighted.

Optimization is not just about rankings on search engines.

Optimization is part of your Omni-channel marketing strategy. You must do everything you can to drive traffic to your website VIA THE SEARCH ENGINES - and not just any traffic but traffic that converts into leads.

To use our P6 client getting recipe model, search engine optimization should always be about getting your offer (i.e. your web page) in front of a potential customer or referral source via a search engine.

If that introduction of your offer to a customer requires you to do something on your site to get your site ranked, that's great. But don't stop there.

ABC's Are Not Just For Nursery School

"Always Be Contacting" other sites to get them to link to or post content about your site because if those sites are getting ranked then you get more chances for people to see your link on those sites and thus drive people to your site - even if it is slightly indirect.

So let's step back for a second and catch a breath.

We started this section by recognizing that there are two types of customers you want to target in any business.

- **Those in the know; and**
- **Those not in the know.**

When we talked about Molly looking online for a Vegan restaurant she is clearly "in the know" because she knows there are vegan restaurants and she just needs to find one.

People like Molly also turn to their friends in Facebook and other similar social sites and to their work colleagues in LinkedIn and other similar professionals only social sites and they simply ask "hey can you recommend a good place to get a veggie burger?"

If Real Food Daily is engaged in a social media marketing strategy, it can generate publicity online and get people to share information about the restaurant and more specifically their cashew cheese veggie burgers.

RFD will be successful if it works through social influencers and bloggers who cover the vegan space online and gets them to endorse the restaurant to their different audiences of followers.

Molly is also likely to use a search engine as a Yellow Pages alternative. And if the restaurant is not optimized even for a search for its name, it can miss out on easy low hanging fruit type of searches when its name fails to show up in the listings.

Open Up More Traffic Channels with PPC

Real Food Daily can get in front of Molly buy bidding on specific keyword phrases using Google Adwords or Bing PPC and pay per click.

Optimizing Real Food Daily itself for search engine rankings makes sense because Molly is likely not the only person looking online for a vegan restaurant. And buying PPC ads could make sense too (if the ROI works out) because the PPC ads come before the organic listings.

And if Real Food Daily has done its keyword research and adopted a strong content marketing strategy, then it will have created a strong lead generation channel to attract people like Molly.

Widen Your Digital Footprint With Social Media Marketing

RFD can also run a Facebook Ad and/or Programmatic Advertising Campaign to reach people based on 300 variations of characteristics like age, marriage status, habits, and hobbies as some examples.

With this kind of pay-per-click advertising on websites and social media feeds that accept ads, you can target individuals on a desktop or laptop PC or on their mobile devices and reach a much larger audience than just the people typing in keyword searches in search engines

The above pathway describes a situation where someone like Molly knows or is confident that a solution exists (i.e. a vegan restaurant) and she may even know the name of the restaurant or that she is looking for a vegan restaurant but she doesn't know how to find the location.

Tease Really Hungry People To Be Aware Of You

I want to revisit the 2nd category of prospects who are "not in the know" and who need to be educated.

We can stick with the vegan restaurant scenario for a moment by focusing on people that are not vegans - not even vegetarians - but are simply looking for really good food or even good healthy food.

This group of people is not looking for a vegan place at all. They are just looking for good or healthy food that other people have endorsed.

Most likely this group of people is going to include a much larger audience than those looking for vegan places.

Everyone wants to find the next hot restaurant or simply a steady winner with good and/or healthy food. And if you remember above my tendency to prefer systems and name brands, I would even suggest naming the Veggie Burger something catchy with a TM symbol.

In this situation, where your prospective customer is not aware that a vegan restaurant exists or that they even could go to a vegan restaurant (to get the best burger), there is an opportunity to create a digital awareness of both the existence of a need and a solution for that need.

You need to get inside people's online conversations and interrupt them with an alert type of messaging strategy that piques their curiosity and says to them:

"Hey, did you know that there are veggie burgers that are just as good as meat burgers?"

If they are interested in a burger, you have now made them stop and think about something they never considered before. And if you repeat this message over and over and someone shares a blog post about this, that person might be bothered enough to check you out more.

Let's go through the math and see how it guides you through a process of attracting interest via search engines or even social media like Facebook.

The first step for Real Food Daily is to pull up the Google Keyword Planner tool we've talked about before so it can see what people are searching for that is relevant to vegan restaurants.

Google Tools Make It So Easy To Compete

The Google Keyword Planner tool presents a totally free and comprehensive report which tells Real Food Daily that there are a substantive number of searches for "great pizza in Los Angeles" and it can optimize its site for these type of non-vegan searches too.

In short, Real Food Daily can dramatically enlarge the scope of its traffic opportunity by adding more keyword phrases into its website content with a broader content marketing strategy approach.

The optimization rules are still the same as for the *vegan* keyword phrases.

It's just going to be more of a challenge to get ranked for more generic phrases because instead of just competing with other local vegan restaurants (and vegan relevant websites), now Real Food Daily will be competing with any local (or chain) restaurant that offers pizza and promotes itself online.

And it will be competing with all the websites that write about pizza or have directories of restaurants that serve pizza.

This gets us back to the beginning of this book.

No one said it would be easy.

My job here is to lay out the architecture of what you'll need to get done if you want sustainable traffic.

Let's review these 2 channels before we get into traffic acquisition strategies.

- When you are trying to attract the audience segments that know what they want, you simply need to get in front of them before they see other offers.

- When you are trying to educate the audience segments that aren't looking for you yet, you need to sidearm your message to them like Kent Tekulvie (of famous Pittsburgh Pirates pitching fame) and get in under their radar by using broader keyword phrasing that could attract them to discover that your business could satisfy their needs too.

Let's catch a breath here because there is some heavy stuff coming up now before we transition into the HOW THE HECK DO I DO ALL THIS part of this book.

To start with, I want to recap the entire P6 recipe structure using our employment law firm scenario. Then we can get into the details of how to get the recipe implemented at the granular level.

As we described above, our case study begins with an employment law firm with a few named partners.

These are the items we know about the law firm:

1. The law practice is located in Louisville, Kentucky.
2. The web address is www.KentuckyFoodLegalGroup.com (KFLG)
3. The firm represents both employers (mostly businesses) AND employees.
4. The firm specializes in the food industry - businesses all the way from the production of the food to the end use restaurant.
5. The managing partner has been practicing law for 25 years.

Keep in mind though that just because there are six ingredients in the recipe, it does not mean that we can just go through each step individually. The ingredients actually work together once you understand the root nature of what you are trying to accomplish.

So you have to have a sort of integrated open mind as you start on your implementation plan. Let me give you an example.

We have said that the first P is PACKAGING the offer. And this refers to multiple things at the same time. Let's pull out the shovel and get some dirt out of the way to uncover what is lying beneath the surface.

Pick a "Lizard Brain" Oriented Domain Name

KFLG knows that it offers employment law services to businesses. In order to successfully design the look and feel and messaging on the website, KFLG can't just display a list of legal practice areas.

To convert more people who land on the website, KFLG needs to "speak to the visitors" and use keyword phrases and nuances that connect with them on a practical and emotional level.

So if you have in mind the rest of the recipe, then you will easily remember that KFLG needs to do audience segmentation research to figure out how it can categorize its client base into identifiable groupings that it can speak to through different content funnels.

What is the critical benefit of doing this audience segmentation in the sense of converting it into a tactical strategy?

The simplest answer is "landing pages" - which is part of the "Packaging" ingredient.

If KFLG identifies an audience segment of restaurants and another audience segment of food distributors look at what KFLG can accomplish.

- KFLG can create two very different landing pages for each of these audiences.
- And the messaging strategy can be completely different based on the NEEDS of each of the audiences.

And that's just the first step.

Once it has these groupings in place, it needs to get into the mindset of each audience.

Restaurants might have high turnover and more accidents as compared to a distribution company that might have employees with more job longevity and who are less prone to workplace accidents.

Create a Navigation Menu and Page Sitemap

By describing its legal services in a way that speaks to each audience through different landing pages,

- KFLG can convince more people in each audience segment to believe that it is uniquely the right firm for them, because,
- KFLG has the experience, the legal team and the local proximity (because its office is in Louisville).

Do you see how all these individual elements form the building blocks of a killer branding strategy that showcases KFLG as the premier employment law firm for companies in the food industry who are in Louisville (or even nearby)?

The more building blocks (i.e. the details behind the 6 P's) you have in your complete digital brand strategy the more likely it is that you will beat any other law firms competing in your space.

By now you should recognize that this is simply about being a better communicator and a more strategic marketer than your competitors.

If you follow this very simple directive of getting inside the minds of each of your target customers, and then creating a navigation experience that speaks to them individually, the yellow brick road will easily appear and lead you directly behind the curtain to the wizard who determines which lawyer to hire.

Connect Intimately with Your Messaging

People love good listeners, right? When you are listening to someone, you are validating that person's feelings.

Wouldn't you agree that if you could make people feel that your website is a "good listener" that they would respond more positively to your offer because you seem more credible and likeable?

So I have this goal I have set out for myself when building a website for a client which is something I describe as "Connecting with the Audience" in its simplest terms. Before you can even think about what to write about and what keywords you need to insert into the website you are going to build, you have to think about the mindset of your clients (current, prospective and future).

Customize Your Solutions to Address Specific Pain Points

Here are the components I believe you should include in a high performance communication strategy that will succeed at transforming prospective leads into existing clients.

1. What are the individual PAIN POINTS you can identify for each audience segment?

2. The more details you can uncover, the stronger you can make your landing pages and overall messaging.

3. What solutions can you provide that address the pain points?

4. Again, it's the same principles. The more details you can provide that individualize your approach for each audience, the more you will keep people interested in your website.

5. What about your background suggests that you are any good at producing a positive outcome?

6. The idea is that just because you are able to do something does not easily translate into you having a fantastic ability to do that thing competently - let alone with excellence.

7. And just because you might be good - think testimonials, years of experience - you still need to communicate that you can:
    a. Act timely
    b. Act responsibly
    c. And bill fairly (even if you are expensive you can still be fair)

Let's put this all together.

Can you transmit something that suggests you are a good listener?

The idea is that you take the time to find out what the client needs - rather than just pulling out your billing time cards and invoice books - and you address these needs with your website content through blog postings, videos, images, testimonials and even surveys.

Just so we are clear, you really have to "Know Your Audience".

This means you have to do research to learn about your different audience segments and their habits, needs, goals, and desires. And part of the segmentation is to create demographic and psychographic profiles which you can use in your landing page copy too.

Address Each Audience Segment Individually

As we complete this section on expansive Audience Segmentation Analysis, I will remind you that there are 4 groups you should always look to communicate with:

- **Current Clients**
- **Prospective Clients**
- **Competitors**
- **Referral Sources (Channel partners and Friends)**

Getting back to our employment law firm, KFLG has identified at least two sets of CLIENT TYPES it wants to reach out to with its website - food distributors and restaurants.

Use Intermediaries to Reach More People

So what should it do next after adding two very compelling landing pages for each of these audience segments to its website? How can KFLG get these 2 landing pages to be promoted and get noticed?

We need to look at a different area of the P6 recipe - which is **getting in front of people again and again**. Truly a separate book can be spent on this topic but we have to commit to something manageable in a short time. Let's unwrap a few ways this can be done at a reasonable budget.

This is a good time to talk about a fantastic method of getting in front of people over and over again.

It is when you can **work through facilitators** that can make introductions that connect you with clients.

I always encourage clients to build more relationships with middlemen – intermediaries.

Look for scenarios with other people that can make digital introductions that connect you with potential clients. That wondrous moment of introduction can be artificially induced and occur with the help of an electronic intermediary:

- A search engine ranking
- A PPC ad
- A website mention (with a link to your site)
- A YouTube video (with a link to your site)
- A blog posting (with a link to your site)

Optimize Your Website for Search Engine Rankings

I want to focus first on search engine marketing because really this is a HUGE ongoing opportunity for service businesses that is just not going away any time soon.

Let's see if we can put some boundaries around this discussion. There are 2 opportunities within the world of search engine marketing:

- **Advertising where you pay per click (PPC) for ads on search engines that are listed in their own area.**
- **Organic rankings where you get ranked for particular keyword phrase searches and don't get charged a PPC cost.**

The advantage of organic rankings is that that a top ranking can give you unlimited clicks that are essentially free (obviously there is an expense to pay for SEO efforts that get you top rankings) as compared to a PPC listing where you pay every time someone clicks on your ad.

I am not going to go into tremendous detail on PPC strategies though there will be a chapter in the Appendix with some ideas to execute.

In reference to organic rankings though, implanting an SEO strategy to grow your rankings is a great way to attract leads from people that are typing in a keyword search thus expressing a need for something they hope to find on a listed website. That is why I want to spend time on SEO tactics.

5 Steps To Become An SEO Aficionado

This book is not going to give you all the details to execute a search engine strategy. BUT, it will give you enough to know what needs to be done. You could actually implement a lot of these tactics. Let's get started with the 5-step TRAPS program for SEO.

SETTING T.R.A.P.S. FOR GOOGLE

A 5-step process that produces an effective and long-lasting search engine rankings result.

> ➤ **T**echnically optimized site with good web coding.

> ➤ **R**elevant keyword phrases appear appropriately.

> ➤ **A**udience connection to increase time spent on site.

> ➤ **P**artner with other websites to link to your site.

> ➤ **S**haring web pages through social channels and blogs.

T.R.A.P.S. includes the five elements above because the main goal of SEO is ultimately to set all these traps that get Google to rank your site which drives people to your site where you can speak to them.

This means you can not only grow your organic rankings but also produce more and better conversions from the people you attract.

The next few pages will include detailed descriptions of the T.R.A.P.S. system and there will also be some articles in the Appendix area that elaborate on this rankings and conversion system even more.

Get "Technical" With On-Page Optimization

  Technical   Relevant   Audience   Partnerships   Sharing

- **The technical side of SEO is known as <u>ON-PAGE Optimization</u>.**
- **This describes all the things that happen INSIDE your website.**

Top On-Page Factors That Affect Your Rankings:

- o Meta tags (including meta title and meta description)
- o Schema architecture that is in the source code of each page
- o The actual web page names used in your URL's
- o Sub-directory folder names and sub-domain names
- o H1-H3 tags –the headlines and sub-headlines on each page
- o Title tags - hidden from the viewer but describe each page
- o The relevant keyword phrases utilized in your content
- o Plugins that are available that can help with SEO goals

Later on in this book I have included explanations of these different on-page factors, with guidelines we recommend for our clients. If you want more details, there are tons of SEO courses and even reading a book like SEO for Dummies is helpful. I can't cover all the nuances of these on-page factors without tripling the size of this book.

What I want to do now is highlight salient points about these tactics so you get a sense of what on-page tactics are all about and at the same time give you some advanced strategies to implement on your site.

Let's go in order of how you would actually get these tactics completed.

You can't get a good web page up without programming it properly. As long as you are already going to hire someone to build your website (or do it yourself) the best thing you can is plan out the coding properly.

Remember our earlier analogy of Plan the Dive, Dive the Plan? This formula works for building websites really well.

Don't Walk Outside Without Your Pants

The first step in planning your commercial website is to develop a blueprint where you architect the ecosystem of your website. This ecosystem includes all the pages you are going to include on the site.

Your Website Probably Includes These Pages:

1. Home page
2. About Your Company page
3. At least one Services page (a more advanced tactic would be to have separate pages for each service you offer)
4. Contact us page (which includes a FORM connected to a database and an autoresponder – not just an email address)
5. Privacy policy (usually pro-forma yet needed for Google)
6. Terms and Conditions (Legally you need this)
7. Optional pages for case studies, testimonials, office locations, news, resources, video gallery and press center.

Just like you don't leave the house until you are dressed, don't launch a website until you have the bulk of your wardrobe of pages planned ahead of time.

A professionally constructed website will also contain a "sitemap" link in the bottom navigation area which links to a page that lists all the pages on the website in a sort of hierarchical layout so that visitors can easily see the structure of the site and find a page more easily.

There is a 2nd type of critical sitemap file that is primarily used by search engines. This is called an XML sitemap.

Get Even More Pages Listed in Google or Bing Search Results

Every website looking for search rankings needs to include this type of sitemap. You can get it for free at www.xml-sitemaps.com by filling out a form. It takes 30 seconds to do this and then maybe a few minutes for the program to run and generate a file you can download also for free.

You are probably wondering what do I do with this XML file.

When you set up a new website, there are two things you need to do before launching it that are critical to its internal performance as well as Google rankings.

1. Visit www.Google.com/Webmaster
2. Visit www.Google.com/Analytics

You need to sign up for an account in both areas. Just follow the instructions. It's a bit technical so ask your website developer to do this for you if it is confusing. DO NOT FORGET THESE 2 STEPS.

Don't accept approval of your website from your web developer without both these items being installed and activated.

Note that you will need a GMAIL address or a Google APPS email (this is basically GMAIL for your business that is a paid and better version of GMAIL) in order to apply for both accounts.

Once you have been approved for a Webmaster account, there is an area to upload your sitemap.xml file that you created earlier.

Here is an advanced tactic we recommend - that must be done manually - since it cannot be automated inside Google Webmaster.

Generate the above XML sitemap file at least once a month (if you create new content) and upload it to your Webmaster account so you can tell Google about the new pages on your site.

Measure Success With Real-Time Reporting Tools

The other item you need in your website is the Google Analytics code which must be installed on every page of your site. *Again, don't accept completion of your website until this is working on your site.*

Analytics offers free reporting that tells you things about your website activity such as where your visitors are coming from and how many pages are being visited.

There are hundreds of Google Analytics report scripts and articles online that give you preformatted custom reports you can use to evaluate your website performance. It's really important to know how your site is doing in regards to bounce rates, time on site and the path people follow from the moment they enter until the exit.

Ok. Getting back to the Sitemap goal in the general sense.

Now that you have a framework for the first set of pages in your website, the next step is adding layers to this foundation.

For SEO and conversion purposes, you need to start expanding your digital footprint by adding more contextually relevant pages.

Chapter 7: A Content Approach to SEO

The Marriage Of "Relevance" And "Context"

T.R.A.P.S.   Technical   Relevant   Audience   Partnerships   Sharing

What topics would you write about and what pages and blog posts would you add as part of your T.R.A.P.S. approach?

First, you have to identify the keyword phrases to include in your content. You have to study the clients who are going to need your services. They type specific phrases into search engines to find someone like you. If you know those phrases your job is half done.

There are two components to the "Relevancy" factor of the TRAPS program.

- First is doing the research to find the keyword phrases people would be typing in as search queries to find a company like yours.
- Second is the context of the conversation those keywords get wrapped inside as part of your sales and value messaging.

Remember, your content muse wants you to write pertinent and compelling content for the different clients you need and want.

Your sitemap concern guides you to designing an ecosystem of a website architecture, but the mandate of "relevancy" requires you to include specific keyword phrases inside pages that contain content that would be interesting to the clients and referral partners you are targeting.

Before looking seriously at describing the services you offer and considering what topics you are going to write about, I recommend looking at your competitors to see what they say about what they do.

You can look at local competitors or just companies that provide similar services even if they are in different cities and don't compete with you directly. Your goal is to build a best practices guide that includes the ideas being implemented by relevant business in your marketplace.

Start taking notes on these topics:

- How are other sites listing and explaining their services
- What headlines are they using on each page
- What types of blog topics are they writing about
- Do they have videos and what kind of videos
- What keyword phrases do you see appearing again and again
- Do you see similar messaging on different sites
- Do they publicize case studies or victories
- Do they offer up testimonials and client reviews
- What external websites are they linking to
- What awards are industry associations are they displaying

The "best practices" approach is sort of like doing research to write a term paper and gives you a framework that you will use to get inside the mindsets of your intended audience targets.

See the sites your prospects view online - that they get referred to or stumble upon. Discover what they are looking for. Preempt their questions with a messaging strategy that differentiates you and elevates your credibility, likability and overall reputation.

Your Services Page Is Vital To Brand Differentiation

One of the main areas services firms are going to tackle first in their differentiation process is the SERVICES section. We find that the SERVICES section is treated as an afterthought - in the sense that it simply lists the services the company can provide to its clients.

Here is an example from a valuations firm that has a link in its top navigation menu which simply says "Services":

- Mergers & Acquisitions
- Fairness Opinions
- ESOP Valuations
- Business Investment

- Sale of a Business
- Succession Planning
- IP Valuations
- Goodwill Valuations
- Bank Financing
- Stock Options Valuation

Seriously, this type of services list does not make a serious attempt to communicate with prospective clients. It's just a laundry list.

At a minimum the link could have said "Valuation Services" because clearly, the firm offer valuation services. Instead, it just said services.

Technically this site fails to communicate as well as it could and should.

This is what we call a FLASHER type of web site.

This is the person in the trench coat walking on the street or in the park, who opens up the coat and says "Hey, look at what I've got."

There is no story here. There's no dialogue.

There's not even a build up to the end result.

It's almost as if the flashing episode never happened because the usual reaction to the flasher is to avert your eyes. Is this the type of negative reaction you want to engender with your website copy?

Be More Than A One Night Stand!

Contrast the flasher story with a well-known seductress tale.

In the story of Salome and the Dance of the Seven Veils, there is a story being told, one veil at a time.

The story has music, it has stages, it has visual imagery with the clothing and the dancer.

In short, this story has TEXTURE.

It has sex appeal ... It's alluring ... It's captivating.

It draws you in and keeps you interested.

Expand your sitemap and extend your website footprint by adding these types of pages.

1. Individual service pages for each type of service offering
2. Industry pages that talk about proficiency in different industries.
3. Case study pages (or sections on other pages) that can accompany specific services and/or industry expertise.
4. Geographically relevant pages that speak to your locale specific relevance. If you have offices in different neighborhoods or cities or states, create separate pages to showcase your connection in each place. Don't just list your address. Do more to show you matter locally.
5. Testimonials from clients. The two birds with one stone move here is to quote a client AND a job position. The reason is that you are name dropping a company and connecting personally with a website visitor who might have a similar job title.

I am not suggesting your website needs to be erotic.

There is a tangible difference between displaying a naked list of services versus investing time to invite someone into your services empire with appealing headlines, captivating images and separate pages for each individual service area that speaks to a unique value and appeal.

Each web page can be presented like a veil in the dance that is going on (whether you like it or not) between your site and the visitor's instinctive response to avert his or her eyes from what you are flashing.

This is why sites have reduced the amount of text on their home pages. They want to dangle compelling headlines with attractive images that aggressively grab your attention and move you into the sales funnel where they can present their story to you one screenfold at a time.

Let's recap for a moment where we are with the TRAPS system.

- You've constructed a website with good coding.
- You've identified a sitemap of pages that should be included.
- You've built a keyword phrase list to embed into your content.

You need to create pathways for visitors to "get stuck" mozying around your site. Not stuck like on flypaper but stuck like licking a tootsie roll.

Designing and Writing To Engage Your Audience

Here is where we can introduce the 3rd ingredient of the TRAPS system which is Audience Engagement.

From an SEO perspective, you want people who land on your site to stay on your site. Whether it's people staying on the entry page or moving to internal pages, the search engines measure the time spent on your site and how quickly people land and leave as well.

This stage of TRAPS is where you have the opportunity to take all that wonderful keyword research that has been built into a keyword list and write good web copy that connects your brand messaging to your audience and keeps them engaged on the site.

And because you used keyword phrases in your web copy that Google is tracking and measuring, you've taken a very big step in the SEO war to position your website for rankings.

Sure there are more steps to accomplish to eventually get ranked but take it to the bank that writing keyword rich copy on a continuing basis is a worthy investment.

Don't Be Monte Hall. Give Visitors Clarity Not Multiple Choices

This makes for a good transition from the relevancy discussion above.

As good as your content might be (both from a keyword standpoint for search engine rankings and from an audience standpoint in terms of relevancy) a linking structure and navigation system is really a more intelligent way of saying "I want to provide people with an intuitive way of getting from page to page as they use my site to find the information they need."

I tend to focus a lot on creating an intuitive way to help people move through your site. The less clicks it takes to get people to the pages they need, the better your site will perform in terms of time spent on site and lower bounce rates.

To be clear, I am not just talking about a navigation menu, but also where you put links inside your web content.

You have to not only write with the intent of connecting your messaging but also link with the intent of moving people along certain pathways.

Let's say you have a page about succession planning which naturally invites discussions about inheritance taxes or life insurance, you should be strategic about linking out to other pages on those two topics (whether they are pages on your site or pages on another site that make you look better for linking to them).

And if you are thinking, did Jason just say to "link to pages outside my site"? The answer is yes because one of the hidden secrets to search engine rankings is that you can actually lend authority to your website by linking to other strong, relevant and/or authoritative websites.

Let's just say it never hurts to link to Wikipedia or other authoritative (that means really powerful) sites.

Getting back to the main point of Audience Engagement, if you can keep people who came from a search engine moving forward inside your site, Google tracks this and your rankings go up.

Your site is not Let's Make A Deal. Don't put people in a situation where they have to guess what is behind each door if they click on a link.

Be Hypnotic With A Visual Navigation Menu

Since we are talking about navigation, I want to suggest something subtle you can do with a drop down or slide-out menu in a navigation bar which can help you broadcast messaging about your services.

For example, a navigation menu item might say "Legal Services." When the users put their mouse over the word Legal Services, a new menu can appear which lists each of your legal services before they click through.

A legal services list like this tells the visitors that you have a specialty in each of those services. Visitors (with his/her own unique situation) can then click on the legal service that looks like it addresses what they need.

And, because you have created a single page for each service, and spent the time to write up some relevant keyword rich text on that page and given it some rich context, you will have more chances to get ranked for those pages AND those pages will perform better in terms of keeping people engaged instead of bouncing.

Sticks And Stones And Naming Conventions

I would like to talk about how you name things on your website:

1. The name of a directory (or folder) in a URL
2. The name of the web page in the URL
3. The text you see in a link (called anchor text)

In the context of the valuations firm I mentioned above, the owner has 2 categories of services - with one category of services being focused mostly on valuations. It is likely that there would be a link on the website that looks like this "valuation services" and points here:

Example: www.ValuationFirmLA.com/valuation-services/index.html

The part of the link above which includes "valuation-services" is technically a directory as far as search engines are concerned. The words "valuation services" underlined above are called anchor text.

Any time you see a slash (/) in a link, it connotes another directory like a folder inside a drawer of a filing cabinet.

The difference between files in a filing cabinet and pages in a website is that if you have multiple references inside a link separated by slashes (e.g. www.ValuationFirmLA.com/valuation-services/miami/hedgefund/) then it's like having a folder inside a drawer that is inside another drawer that is also inside another drawer.

The optimization guidelines used to be different. Now, the less "drawers" (i.e. directories) you have in links, the better your SEO results.

Plus, for conversion purposes - especially with the proliferation of mobile phone usage - shorter links are easier to share and easier to type into a phone or tablet device thus making them more friendly.

These SEO rules also guide how you should be naming of pages.

Though shorter page names are better, you still do better if you can insert keyword phrases into your page names.

Note that in the "hedgefunds" link example above, the way the URL is constructed, Google knows from the link structure that the page is related to the valuation services section of the website which sort of leads to a catch-22 though in terms of what is a better link.

In one sense a short link (e.g. www. ValuationFirmLA.com/hedgefunds) is preferable, but in another sense you want the context of the hedge fund page being associated with the valuation services category.

The jury is out here on a best practice though.

The compromise seems to be to have the **/valuation-services/** as a category page (that lists links to each services page) and possibly even have the subcategory page of **/Miami** but only use the shorter link to the actual page without all the category and subcategory references.

To be honest this stuff is confusing even to me as I write this. Talk to your web developer to review options. Just don't ignore this.

Getting A Handle On "Anchor Text"

This is a BIG BIG deal. It crosses over into multiple areas of SEO. Let's talk about how to use anchor text for content ON the pages of your site.

There are two benefits to being more verbose with your anchor text.

- First, is that Google will see that your services are actually "legal" services. That automatically puts you ahead of any other site that just uses the term services.

- Secondly, for the website visitor, the term "legal services" will jump out faster and catch attention more than a pedestrian term of just "services". This can reinforce the message that this website is being provided by a firm that offers specific legal services.

The first area is inside your navigation menu. You could simply have a link in your menu that says "Services" or you could have a link that says "Legal Services."

The same approach to your navigation menu can also be used with the links in your drop down menu as well as with other links in your website. Under the legal services menu item, you could have links to services pages that are more descriptive too such as "employee handbook policies" instead of "policies" alone.

There is one other aspect of anchor text to deal with and it concerns percentages - or in plainer terms how many times you use the same anchor text for links pointing to your site and pointing inside your site.

Stay Away From Anchor Text Spamming

If you have too many links with the same anchor text choice, the Google looks at the links and starts thinking that you are spamming the search engines with artificially created links. One of the challenges with organic rankings is that your SEO tactics have to look natural. Once the search engines get an idea that you are essentially doing too much and too fast to gain rankings, they start to withdraw support.

It's time for a deep breath.

This on-page stuff and linking rules are not only complex in terms of all the variables at play, it's also pretty damn boring. I wish there were a way to jazz this stuff up. There really isn't. You just have to trudge through it step by step. And truthfully, this book could not do justice to the full range of options available simply with structuring links and pages on your site.

What I hope to accomplish though is to give you some ideas for you to explore with whoever is managing your website promotion strategies. And if you are not promoting your website, then at least you have some guidelines for things you can start looking into and maybe get encouraged to start investing more resources here.

Meta-Tags For Dummies

Let's keep going while the iron is hot and press on with some more on-page tactics. **Let's talk about meta-tags.** This area is going to be much easier.

There are two primary meta-tags to embed onto every page of the site:

- The meta-title, and
- The meta-description

The Meta-Title is the title of your page that Google sees when it "reads" the source code of your page. The guidelines for the length of each tag continues to change so I can't give you a rule now. Look it up online.

Here's the thing. For your benefit I am not digging deep to explain certain things in major detail because it's easy enough to go to any search engine and simply look up the description of a meta-title and how to apply it to your website content and programming.

META TITLE AND META DESCRIPTION GUIDELINES:

In regard to each meta-title, what you want to include in under 60 characters is a description that accomplishes two purposes:

1. It describes what the page is about.
2. It uses keyword phrases that closely match what someone would type into Google to discover the page you are writing about.

In regards to a meta-description, the goals are fairly similar.

1. The length of the description can be 130 characters.
2. You need to use complete sentences that are grammatically correct. Note that Google often uses some of your meta-description as the text it displays below your organic listing.

What I want to accomplish is to highlight which features you need to ensure are included in your website - and this can simply mean that you need to ensure your web developer takes care of them.

Here is one last instruction that comes into play when you are dealing with meta-tag optimizations. It's called the Header tag which is something actually visible on your website to each visitor.

The header tag comes in 3 format known as H1, H2 and H3. H1 is the first main headline and H2 is a sub-headline and H3 is another sub-headline.

Use the tags multiple times on a page but only use H1 one time.

Think of the H1 header as the main headline that tells the visitor what the page is all about. And all the main content on the page that follows the headline should have semantic keyword phrases that bolster the context of what the headline is presenting.

Captivating Headlines Set The Tone For Maximum Performance

As an example, a good headline for the Valuation Firm would be "Hedge Fund Valuation Services". And if the firm has an office in Miami, an even better headline is "Hedge Fund Valuation Services in Miami."

I think there is value in distinguishing two types of pages of content - especially in regards to headlines and page names.

- A page that describes a service or practice area really just needs to tell the visitor what the page is about. And if there is geographic relevance, mention that too.

- The hedge fund title above works great for conversion and for SEO simply because it clarifies what the page is about and sets the tone for the content that follows.

- A blog post though is designed to stimulate interest and engender a response. A provocative title such as "10 Unexpected Ways to Maximize Your Hedge Fund Valuation" would be great for a blog post because it begs to be clicked and shared.

A blog is a great place to utilize hypnotic content writing even though you sacrifice some of the keyword goals in your headlines.

You can more than make up for the lack of keywords in a blog title by inserting all the relevant keyword phrases into the actual blog post.

You can also bump up the blog value if you get a link on a page on another strong website that links to you. The link on the other website sets the stage for Google to "Expect" relevant content on your site - even if the headline is not very keyword rich.

Here's something important when you consider what to insert in your Header and Meta tags. It used to be for SEO purposes, you would want the Meta-title, Meta-description and H1 tags to have very similar information.

Google has gotten smarter. It wants to see variations in your web content so that it looks more natural as opposed to contrived.

Here's my advice for now in regards to Headers and Meta-tags. Make sure they are not identical. Use your brand name in the Meta-Title tag. And for your description, write full readable sentences - especially since you have more space under the guidelines.

Since we have been talking about strategic usage of keyword rich text, we might as well close this section out by transitioning into guidelines for the content in your web copy.

Be More Impactful Than A Pimple On An Elephant

You cannot just embed any keyword phrases in headlines and meta-tags unless those keyword phrases ALSO appear in the body text of those pages too. And that's not all.

You also need SEMANTIC TEXT in your website content - which refers to related phrases that the search engines (and people too) expect to show up as being relevant to the primary meta-title.

I'll share an example.

If you are writing a page about the horse racing season, then a human reader would expect to see other words on the page such as jockey, race track, betting, and pari-mutuel.

If the Google spider (that mimics a human reader) finds words like Black Stallion and does not see a healthy mix of those other relevant racing terms, then Google is going to grade your web page as NOT relevant to racing - even if you had racing terms in your title, description and header tags.

Here are some other guidelines for embedding keyword rich content into your website.

First is that you can insert keyword phrases into all these content areas:

1. Video file names
2. Image names
3. Document names (like Powerpoint or PDF)
4. The anchor text of links to other websites like Wikipedia
5. Any text format including sentences, paragraphs and lists.
6. Put a primary phrase in an H1 header tag
7. Put secondary phrases in H2 and H3 header tags
8. Inside page links use the "title" tag to put keywords
9. Inside image links use the ALT tag to insert keywords too.

If you are thinking about what is an appropriately sized page of web content to write or blog post to publish, there are differing opinions. Certainly, the longer a page you have the more keywords you can write about that are related to each other.

I think the guideline should not be the search engines. Rather it should be what is going to keep someone on the page for a long time. And get that person to take the action you want to be taken.

If your conclusion is to have a video with a sentence or two of introduction, then just get the keywords to be spoken inside the video and annotate the video to include the keywords "behind the scenes" in the video code. See the article in the Appendix by Richard Clayman about using videos to promote your business.

If you conclude that people will suck up any information you provide, then put out a whitepaper or a 2,000 word post and make it the end all be all of that particular topic. Google tends to love this kind of context rich content. And if you can get it socially endorsed, which I will be covering soon, then you can get an ever greater boost.

There is more to discuss in regards to optimizing your body content but for the purposes of this guide, you definitely have enough to be dangerous now. For more advanced tactics, check out my company blog. We always have some good references there.

The Best Scheme Is HTML "Schema"

There is one final item to cover in our technical on-page SEO section - and this is SCHEMA ARCHITECTURE.

When you access your Google webmaster account, there is a section in the administration menu that talks about markup text. This is a way of using structured coding to tell Google's search engine spider what certain sections of the page are about.

Think of markup text as a back door into Google. It's the password you keep in your desk drawer. Everyone knows it's there but people tend to leave it there untouched. Well open the drawer and embed schema architecture into your site.

Again, I am not going to get into the specifics here. Just talk to your web developer or get an article from a Google search that talks about embedding schema data into your web pages.

Let's do a quick review of where we are in the TRAPS system.

1. You have done keyword research to build a list of phrases.
2. You have studied competitors and have a best practices guide.
3. You have technically optimized the website coding and content.
4. You have embedded keyword rich content intelligently.
5. Your content reduces bounce rates and keeps people engaged.
6. You have created a linking architecture that enables visitors to move from page to page with ease.

Great. Let's move forward onto getting rankings because here is the big fallacy with search engine optimization that I probably have to explain in every client meeting where SEO is on the agenda.

Chapter 8: Grow Organic Rankings By Being Popular

Introducing The Power of Backlinks

I assume that everyone has read a book or two on optimization and has done all the above items. I assume that every one of my clients' competitors has invested some amount of resources into complying with the ON-PAGE guidelines we have been framing.

These assumptions thus lead me to conclude that any competitor of my client that I have to be worried about is naturally going to have a keyword rich and content heavy website that is technically in good shape.

If all these assumptions are correct and I look at my client and all their effective competitors as being effectively equal in this regard, then how is Google going to separate my client from the pack.

Since many of my meetings tend to happen in restaurants or coffee shops like Coffee Bean, it's really easy to visualize this problem by using a handful of sugar packets.

This is how the conversation always seems to go.

I reach over to the container of sugar packets and I pull out one of them and as I lay it down the on the table, I say "this is your website." I then reach over and pull out another 3 or 4 of the same sugar packets and I say as I lay each one down, "these are your effective competitors" and they have all read the same SEO books and written the best SEO content too.

I then reach over and pull out a Splenda (or Equal) packet and lay that one down above the other packets and say "how does Google choose your brown sugar packet over all the other highly optimized brown sugar packets and treat you like a Splenda packet" - and give you higher rankings?

The answer is popularity - or more technically backlinks.

This is where we start the discussion of backlinking or what I will later describe in the TRAPS system as PARTNERING with other sites.

To be clear, I am not talking some secret partnership with other sites. I just like the terminology of PARTNERING rather than backlinking because I think it really highlights the goals you need to achieve and a mindset that will help you achieve them.

Where Do Backlinks Come From?

A backlink simply refers to a link that appears on another website that links to your website.

How do you get a backlink?

There are many ways to get a backlink. Here are some examples:

1. Someone is asked for free to link to your website.
2. The site owner is paid (whether money or some other exchange of value) to link to your website. This is called black hat.
3. You build a different website and link that one to your first website. (this could be considered grey hat)
4. You submit a form online that posts the information (including a link to your website) on someone else's website.
5. The site owner discovers your web page and volunteers to link to it (this is what Google wants to see happen naturally).

There are hundreds of techniques to get quality backlinks.

The above examples are a framework you can reference that describes many different variations of how to acquire backlinks to a website.

Here's the core rule in regards to backlinks and rankings.

The more links you get on websites that are contextually relevant to your website AND that are themselves considering to be AUTHORITATIVE (read this to mean powerful) by Google's measurements, the higher your rankings will climb.

This process of building backlinks is also referred to as OFF PAGE optimization. Websites that want to increase their organic rankings in a competitive marketplace must grow the backlinks to their sites.

Backlinks Are Not Democratic

It's important to understand that this urgency to grow links is not like a traditional election where you need to accumulate as many votes as you can get by a certain point in time.

First of all you have to keep acquiring backlinks pretty much forever. Secondly, votes are not treated equally. The value of each votes is NOT the same.

A backlink from a legal blog post on CNN or an article by a lawyer on Huffington Post is simply far more powerful to a law firm website than a link on a health and wellness site from a guy in his garage who has little traffic or engagement with his content.

SEO companies are constantly on the prowl to find ways to acquire links for their clients that look natural and don't cost too much to acquire.

Of course this idea of costing too much is a relative concept because if you spend $5,000 on efforts to get an article published on a site like CNN with a backlink, it could very well be worth that sum.

You may be wondering how a backlink can have a cost associated with it if Google's guidelines strictly point out that you should not pay websites for backlinks.

Let's use our employment attorney in Kentucky to illustrate an answer.

Our client has written a blog post on a trend in the restaurant scene in Kentucky where waiters are stealing silverware because there is a shortage of silver (ok, It's a wacky example but it caught your attention didn't it).

What we need to do from a search engine rankings perspective is reach out to other websites that have content that is relevant to this topic and let these sites know about my client's new article. And, my goal is to get these sites to post something about the article and link to the article from their website.

I have two intertwined goals here. First, is to get contextually relevant sites to link to the article. Second, is to get powerful sites that may not be very contextually related but their power translates into what is called LINK JUICE when they put a backlink on their site to my client's site.

So where does the cost of a backlink come from?

Simply it's a labor cost to identify and then reach out to these sites. Many companies simply can't afford to execute these type of outreach services. It's why public relation firms are so expensive because the bulk of their work involves finding and connecting with people that can publish.

The Pursuit of Backlinks Reframed As A Virtual Partnership

If you do research on backlink tactics, you will see that there are all sorts of ways you can get backlinks from other sites. Some kosher, some not so kosher. Some free and some not so free.

I want to talk about PARTNERING with other sites not from an actual "reach out and contact them standpoint" but rather from a "mindset" standpoint where the backlinks will flow naturally because of the content you are guided to create in this partnering mindset process.

If we all agree that rankings (in a competitive environment) are impacted by quantity and quality of your backlinks (i.e. LINK JUICE), then it also means we can agree that if you give a someone a good reason to link to your website it might be easier to get the link.

If you start thinking about what you could do as a GOOD PARTNER for these other websites to provide THEM with value, you may start finding them more willing to link to you – thus, an easier pathway to backlinks.

Let me give you an example.

ACQUIRING BACKLINKS STARTS WITH IN-DEPTH RESEARCH:

Instead of thinking first about the topic you want to write about because you see something trending in BuzzFeed, look instead for powerful sites that would be great to get backlinks from and see what kind of content they are publishing and promoting.

As you evaluate the themes within their website content and the audiences they are engaging, consider what type of content you could create for them that would induce the Pavlovian response you need - a request by them to link to your site.

If you view yourself as a joint venture partner to other websites, you will likely create keyword rich content you already need but have it geared for distribution on other sites simply because your content will be more resonant to their needs.

Here's a super fragilistic type of secret way to find the topics you can write about that will get shared more often. It's so simple that it got a brand name associated with it. I will present a variation of it here.

For reference purposes you can look up the term skyscraper content on Google from Brian Dean to see more on this technique.

Content Should Stick Out Like A Skyscraper And Be Noticed

Find an article that has been shared a lot and that has a lot of views. Obviously look for a topic that is relevant to your business. Put together your own version of that article. I don't mean copy it. I mean write something on the same topic but with your own perspective.

One of the statistically proven and best pieces of content you can write for this purpose is a top 10 list. You don't need to stick to 10. Just make a top something list and that will be usually be more popular than a non-list type of content piece. You can also create this same content in the form of a video or image slideshow and then load it up on YouTube or Slideshare.

You can even find someone else's top 10 list and write your own top 15 list incorporating the ideas from the top 10 list. Just give appropriate attributions and put a spin on the top 15 list with your personal flavor.

Before you actually publish the article or top 10 posting on your site, you need to put the tease in place. It's almost like being Robert Redford in the Sting. You need to reach out to at least 5 or 10 of the websites (and their owners) that shared the original article you found. Connect with them and let them know you are putting out something that might resonate with their readers. This technique is a great - though - labor intensive way to build your backlink arsenal.

One other type of content you could create is an "infographic" which is a visually better way of writing about statistical date. Look it up on Google. We create them for clients even though they take up to 10 hours to produce. But the value is great because people like this type of content.

Remember Your Kindergarten Lessons on Sharing?

T.R.A.P.S.   Technical   Relevant   Audience   Partnerships   Sharing

This last point about writing and sharing infographics is a great transition point to the last ingredient of the TRAPS organic rankings system which is getting your content SHARED.

If you look back at the TRAPS system, it has involved a few core tactics:

1. Put keyword phrases inside a technically "optimized" website
2. Write targeted content that keeps people on your site
3. Grow your Authority by continuously getting good backlinks

There is a fourth ingredient that brings everything together in one nice bow because it creates a sort of circular effect that keeps the system going and going long after you publish your content.

This ingredient is technically described as "content sharing" but can also be referred to as "social adoption" in social marketing channels.

The more that people like, follow, share and retweet your web pages and other content inside your website and outside (but connected to) your website (e.g. Facebook updates, YouTube channel videos, Tweets, Pinterest boards, Flickr image galleries) the more your rankings will get impacted.

The substance of your social engagement tells the search engines that people like what you are saying through your digital channels. Imagine that you publish a blog post today and it is still getting circulated months from now through other social channels and blogs. Don't you think this lends credibility to the value your blog post content contains?

SEO companies are investing heavily to expand their agencies to offer social media marketing services because clients now get two benefits for the same cost. In addition to being able to stimulate social engagement which produces its own direct traffic to your website, if we are successful at promoting your content via social media marketing, we are able to impact your search rankings at the same time.

Putting This Book Into Perspective So I Can Grab Some Dinner

I have missed way too many dinner time meals writing this book because as much as the ideas are crystal clear in my head, when you put them on paper they start sounding like a whoopee cushion.

I am sure without much effort I could write hundreds of pages on attracting more clients with search engine ranking and social media engagement strategies. But that has not been my purpose.

As I set out at the beginning of this relatively quick read (I hope), I wanted to tackle a mindset and an approach to getting more clients.

Rather than overwhelm you with a list of tactics to implement as you grow your lead funnel I have endeavored to do what I learned in Law School. Present a few case studies that give me an excuse to present the ideas I want to convey but also give me the ability to sneak in some tactics along the way - under your radar too.

First and foremost, my inclination is to help you understand that the secret to growing your business is not in a faraway unknown galaxy but rather pretty close if you just know where to look.

Sure, you have to invest more than you expected to design, build and lay out a professional looking web site that gives your professionally priced billing rates meaning, legitimacy and substance.

Sure, you need to spend time writing (or hiring good writers) ongoing keyword rich content that can attract search engine traffic while giving YOU an excuse to tout your strengths and drop some names.

Sure, you need to swallow a big pill and invest in a concerted effort to get your content distributed to other websites that can both impact your rankings and drive direct traffic to your website.

Sure, you might even go the extra mile to taking some risk and advertising online in YouTube or Google Adwords or Bing PPC ads or even Facebook ads.

But ask yourself this really painful question.

If you don't make these righteous investments in your digital brand presence, are you comfortable with handing over all this new business to competitors who are going to position themselves ahead of you and take away the leads that are rightfully yours?

I am not comfortable with it which is why I wrote this book.

What's your next move master Luke?

Pax Vobiscum. Shalom.

Jason

Appendix 1: Reviewing the Goals And Purpose of Your Website

This article is a recap of part of the P6 recipe viewed through the lens of using a website to publicize your brand and attract more leads.

How do you position yourself to attract clients and grow referrals?

After reading much of this book, you now know that you start with an "industry assessment" where you learn about your clients, referral sources and competitors. Your goal is to understand what needs exist for your services and find effective ways to articulate how you can address those needs with solutions you can provide. And your web site and social properties have to do the job of engaging these 3 audience groups and setting you apart from competitors.

Once you have completed your industry assessment and gained a deeper understanding of your business, this is when you put together an internal policy paper where you record the things you want to say and identify the different audiences you want to address.

Since this book is about digital market penetration – i.e. reaching out to current and prospective customers online – I am proposing that your first meaningful step in your marketing strategy is to design and create a web-based vehicle for this engagement dialogue – i.e. a website.

Essentially this means you will need a full web presence strategy that includes a professionally designed website along with matching social media profiles (Facebook, Twitter, YouTube and Linkedin, and quite possibly a Google Plus page too, if only for SEO purposes).

Your Web Presence Viewed As An Orchestral Arrangement

All these web properties should work together in concert to create a digital brand environment whose purpose is to convert visitors into leads and referral sources for your service business.

Every element of content on your website or social media page or even a newsletter you send via email or an article you get published on some other website or blog has one single purpose – to introduce your brand value to the reader and move that reader along a chain of trusting and believing you can solve a problem reliably and in an expected time frame – and perhaps better than a competitor.

When I was a practicing CPA, we learned about the doctrine of the 4 corners which suggested that any page of work product we delivered would have to stand on its own 4 corners. I think a web page has to abide by the same guidelines albeit with different rules.

I have sought to identify 3 three challenges (think back to the three gatekeepers example earlier in this book) that your web copy messaging needs to overcome in order to subtly help people to drop their guard, stay on the page they are on and allow themselves to be sold by you.

The first method to keep someone from quickly hitting the back key and bouncing off your website is to showcase what your site is about so it's clear what you do. As an example, this type of messaging can include listing your professional services or listing the problems you address with your services or solutions. This type of clarity helps the reader (who has a problem) make a decision that this page might have something valuable to offer since the page is talking about something he or she invariably might need.

The second technique to keep someone from hitting the back key and leaving your site is to highlight your brand value proposition[s]. The idea here is to start the process of setting you apart from other providers and build this notion that you are really good at what you do and that you have experience working with people in similar situations.

This approach is a nuance to the first method because instead of talking about what you do, you are now talking about who you do it for. In a sense, you could say it's another side of the coin, but you could also say that talking to a CFO is not the same as talking to a CEO, even if the problem is the same. Both people have different motivations.

The last technique to keep someone engaged AND get them to pull the trigger and reach out to connect with you, is the more intangible goal of Inspiring them to trust and believe you are the BEST solution to their need. This is about a lot more than being perceived as a credible and reliable provider. This is about being better than the rest.

Here is a list of content strategies we talked about in the book that you can utilize in your marketing plan. Display the following items:

- Case studies of success stories
- Testimonials from happy clients and vendors
- Years of experience doing what you do
- Awards from meaningful sources
- Membership in industry associations with any recognitions
- Video versions of any of the above that you distribute via YouTube

Once your website is live is when the hard work of promoting yourself really begins.

Anyone can really build a website.

Even if you use a free or cheap template or even a Wix type of web site (please don't do that if you are serious about having a substantive online presence), it's pretty easy to get something up online.

What do you do after the site is live?

How do you get traffic to the site?

Go to the next Chapter in this Appendix section as I put it all together.

Appendix 2: Blogging Tactics That Help With SEO

Because search rankings are such a powerful traffic source, one of the most valuable rankings strategies is to add blog posts to your website.

Here are some tangible benefits of writing blog posts or creating video blogs (Vlogs) that engage your potential client base and help you grow the footprint of your brand on the digital landscape.

Write About Relevant and Timely Issues

If your articles cover relevant topics of interest to your current and prospective clients, you can establish your street creds as a "thought leader" in the space - a guru of sorts who has something relevant to say.

Once you achieve the status of being perceived as a thought leader, the perpetual motion effect comes into play as well. Other bloggers and writers will interview you and/or write about your thoughts in their pieces online thus stimulating more interest in what you have to say. And, if they link to you, that gives you a backlink as well which enhances your SEO efforts.

Include Multiple Keyword Phrases In Your Content

If you have followed the P6 strategy and studied your competitors and completed a full keyword research review, then you should already have created a library of keyword phrases that you used when building your website. With your blog, you should pull more phrases from your keyword library and insert variations of them into your blog postings.

The search engine spiders will "index" not just those keyword phrases but ALL the content around these keyword phrases into their databases.

The more blogs you post the more chances you can achieve higher rankings EVEN FOR KEYWORDS you didn't exactly write about.

Every blog you write and every relevant phrase you include is like planting seeds that can blossom over time into multiple search engine rankings that drive visitors to your site.

Attract Subscribers And Attention To Your Blog

If your blog is successful, you can attract loyal followers and subscribers that can automatically receive your blog updates. People can subscribe to your blog using an RSS Feed Reader or you can have people enter their email address and subscribe the old fashioned way and then you can email them as you update your blog.

If you are wondering how this intersects with an SEO effort let me explain. Writing a blog and posting is of course a necessary act. But wouldn't you be better off if that blog post was shared and distributed and liked – especially inside the ecosystem where your client base is living online?

The more people that subscribe to your blog content, the more chances you have they will socially endorse it – by sharing, retweeting or liking it. These social signals give you backlinks possibly and tell the search engines that your content is valued.

What Can You Do To Promote Your Blog?

Go find a popular blog post on a similar topic or written by a competitor or just a blogger that is on topic. See who has commented on that post. See who has shared it or liked it or retweeted. Contact any of these people and say "I've got a piece that you might enjoy since you liked this other article."

With specifically targeted outbound efforts like this, you can find people that would be interested in what you have to say and get your blog quickly syndicated on other websites that have their own visitors. It's not uncommon to spend 50% of the time promoting your blog.

Get More Views With A Facebook "Boost"

One of the most economical ways to promote your blog is to post it to Facebook or Twitter and buy a BOOST. For $5.00 or more, your post can reach thousands of people. Usually it works as a concentric circle starting with your immediate connections. If you boost your post, then the connections of your connections may see the post too.

What Should You Blog About?

To keep a blog alive and thriving, figure out what to write about week after week (or whatever periodic timeframe you commit to). Here are some blog writing tactics that can fuel your publishing strategies:

- Study your competitors' websites, blogs and social media channels.
    - See what they are writing about and their messaging tactics.
    - Who are they addressing in their content strategy?
    - What keywords are they using?

- Use Google Keyword Planner (free in your Google Adwords account) to find groups of keyword phrases to use in your own web content. Pull keywords from other websites using their synonym tool.

- Study "Google Trends" and sites like www.trendspottr.com and BuzzFeed to see what people are talking about and trending topics. Insert popular topics into your keyword goals and your content will be more relevant while still keyword rich for your ranking goals.

- Write or make video content that search engines love and people love too. Here are a few examples:
    - Top 10 lists (any number will do)
    - Top 5 women in "x" industry (or job capacity)

Appendix 3: SEO Rankings Tactics In General

Once your website is live and your blog posting schedule is in place, there are more steps to take to optimize your site. Some of these steps can actually happen while your site and blog are under construction. Just work them out according to your own set of priorities and resource demands.

Perform An Audience Segmentation Analysis

Do an Audience Segmentation Analysis (ASA) to learn about the needs and requirements that exist within your targeted customer base. The more successful you are at using a web page to create a one to one type of dialogue with a prospective client, the more likely that prospect will turn into a lead. Your ASA should guide you to figuring out which audience specific landing pages need to be created and what supporting content will be required to guide readers through your site. Use tools like www.zuumsocial.com to do your research.

Find Keyword Phrases Used In Your Industry

Use the Google Keyword Tool and other keyword research tools (e.g. www.Moz.com) to complete a competitive keyword research analysis. The goal is to identify keyword phrases that closely match what people would be typing into Google and Bing when they do searches and insert those phrases into your web content (pages, blogs, images and videos).

Remember as I covered in the Real Food Daily vegan restaurant case study in Chapter 2 that you always are targeting two different audiences who may need your services:

- People that know there is a solution to a problem
- People that don't know there is a solution, but they have a problem.

See What Sites Are Linking To Your Competitors

Study your competitors' headlines, body copy and videos that they are broadcasting to their audiences. Do a "backlink profile analysis" to find the sites linking to their blog postings and other pages on their sites. You can then contact those websites to see if they will link to your website and/or repost your blog content. There are plenty of link analysis tools that make it easy to see who is linking to a website.

The reason I started this section with a messaging analysis is because if you see themes that get consistently written about by your competitors, you can start writing about those topics as well and attract interest from the same list of site owners which will help your search rankings.

What Should I Do On Facebook?

Build out any social profiles that are good for your business and link them to your website. The first rule of thumb is to match the brand identity to your website and logo. It should not cost more than $500-$750 to have someone design a Facebook landing page and program the HTML code to get it to look like it is part of your corporate identity.

Then you need to start building your audience by getting social endorsements of your content and growing your follower base. The opportunities for free endorsements though have been strictly curtailed in the interest of earnings.

Even if you have 10,000 followers to your Facebook page, if you don't advertise your own status updates by boosting them, you will only reach a fraction of your followers. The point is that you need to budget an advertising cost just to reach your own audience of followers.

The hidden hack here obviously is to find a way to get your Facebook audience to give you their email address so you can reach them via email or some other method that is less costly.

How To Reach People Who Are Not Using Search Engines

In addition to getting free organic rankings, or buying pay-per-click ads that appear in the search engine listings, you can make a list of other Omni-Channel marketing strategies that can expand your reach online. Here are a few traffic channels that bypass the search engines entirely:

- Social media advertising on sites such as Facebook, Twitter, Pinterest, and Instagram. I think of these sites as being more personal social than business social so the types of ads you utilize might be nuanced for those audiences.

- Advertising on more commercially oriented business networks like Yelp, Linkedin and Google Plus. These networks are more geared for advertising because the nature of the usage of the website is for a commercial businesslike function. People go to Yelp to find a service provider that they want to hire. (Restaurants are essentially service providers you hire to cook your meal for you).

- YouTube ads are great because you only pay when people watch the videos. And a visual experience is totally different.

- Programmatic PPC advertising can reach people online using psychographic and demographic profiling parameters. There are 300 characteristics you can use in building an audience targeting model. Your ad campaigns appear on dozens or thousands of websites but only show up when the user fits a specific profile.

  Want to reach pet owners that are married with 3 kids under the age of 20, and who live in specific zip codes? You can do it though you will need to work through an agency.

Appendix 4: SEO Tools and Tips

At the core of any website launch you need to set up these accounts and make sure that your sites are validated. If you want advanced Google Analytics tactics, read this article: www.goo.gl/NaH1Bs

- www.Google.com/Analytics
- www.Google.com/Webmaster
- www.Bing.com/Webmaster

To get free corporate email, I only know of one site that will give you unlimited email addresses with your domain. www.Zoho.com. If you want to use corporate email that is paid, the two most obvious choices are Office365 and Google Apps for Work. I can't speak to the Apple environment but both of these work for iMac just fine.

One of the things this book has covered in great detail is the need to optimize your website. The step-by-step optimization process is called an SEO Audit where you validate that your site has been technically optimized and you uncover the optimization gaps to be fixed.

To do a comprehensive Site Audit of meta-tags, title tags, body content, duplicate content, keyword phrase usage, speed of website, and your backlink profile, you will require analytic software tools. Then you need to fix the problems. This is why an Audit cost can range from $2,500 all the way up to $10,000 depending on the size of the site and the extent of the Audit parameters and deliverables. It's a lot of work.

Here are 3 Freemium and paid web-based tools that are quite useful in doing an SEO Audit. Truthfully we don't recommend you doing the Audit on your own. But if you want to do some research, these tools are great.

- www.MajesticSEO.com
- www.Ahrefs.com
- www.Moz.com

Appendix 5: Backlinks You Can Acquire Easily

To get your website indexed in Google and Bing, Neil Patel suggests in his blog (www.goo.gl/ONmH9T) to add your website URL to these sites:

- For Google: www.goo.gl/RTq4SH
- For Bing and Yahoo: www.goo.gl/JCDkJL

To see if your site has been indexed just go to www.Google.com and type in this search: *site:putyourdomainnamehere.com*

Then, generate an XML sitemap file and upload it into your Google Webmaster account. You can use www.xml-sitemaps.com to create the file or a WordPress plugin here: www.goo.gl/oVD5uX

Next you have to start building up your backlinks and create a credible link profile from relevant and Authoritative sites.

The first step is to add your site or blog URL to these sites.

- http://plus.google.com
- http://www.Youtube.com (add one video linking to your site)
- http://www.vimeo.com (you can add the same video here)
- Set up your blog RSS feed: http://feedburner.google.com/
- http://www.technorati.com
- Add your blog to a category here: http://www.alltop.com
- A list of sites to submit your blog to: www.goo.gl/LYDwwC
- Register for www.Tumblr.com and www.StumbleUpon.com

The next step is to add your company name and physical address to these CITATION directories. You may not be able to add your website address but it is still ok because the search engines are smart enough to associate the physical address with your website.

- www.Yelp.com

Appendix 6: WordPress Tactics and Things Not To Screw Up

- Robots.txt file. Don't block pages from being indexed in error.
  - Here is a testing tool: www.goo.gl/1gXEPE
  - Here is another Google tool: www.goo.gl/XkjuWq

- Your mobile friendliness status: www.goo.gl/5B0meu

- Set images to all be stored in one directory instead of adding a new folder for each month and year. (Settings > Media)

- If you redo your website and you delete or change how pages are named and/or what directories they are in, you must set up 301 redirects. I have included a plugin link below.

- Add these plugins into your WordPress site:
  - Custom permalinks: www.goo.gl/cAi8hY
  - Admin Dashboard manager: www.goo.gl/cf8BtM
  - HTML Editor: www.goo.gl/SUQFxd
  - Disable comments: www.goo.gl/0bjrjh
  - Image replacer: www.goo.gl/Hv5Qc
  - WordPress XML Sitemap too: www.goo.gl/S4Pj6H
  - 301 Redirections: www.goo.gl/60Uy2a
  - Yoast for SEO: www.goo.gl/MvWXfy

- Specific content elements to embed in your site:
  - Big phone number on your mobile site.
  - Vanity phone number (for branding purposes)
  - Call to actions on every page to invoke a response
  - Use smart forms to help people fill them out.
  - Use Captcha on forms to avoid spam

Appendix 7: Leveraging Human Capital To Get Introductions

Work through facilitators that can make introductions that connect you with authority to prospective clients. I always encourage clients to build more relationships with middlemen – intermediaries. The primary reason that this works is that an introduction enables you to skip many steps in the trust building process. If someone whose opinion counts makes a referral, you basically just have to show up on time and not act like a buffoon and you can land the new client and close the deal.

In addition to just building out your business network and waiting for random introductions from people that have come to know, like and trust you, consider formalizing an intermediary relationship. Offer to pay a commission or some other form of quid pro quo in order to induce and/or inspire the intermediary to make more introductions.

I can make a pitch here for the www.Provisors.com business network in Chapter 2. It started in Southern California and is expanding to Boston and Chicago. If you don't have a Provisors group nearby, look for a high grade referral network and join it. Not only will you gain referrals, but you will improve your own pitch as you meet more and more people and have to talk about your business at meetings.

Look for scenarios with intermediaries that can make DIGITAL introductions. Expand your thinking here. The concept of an endorsed electronic introduction could include any of these methods:

- An email introduction with an endorsement
- A conference call with an introduction
- A search engine ranking (your listing is endorsed by Google)
- A PPC ad (same thing but more valued since you paid for it)
- A website mention or social comment (with a link to your site)
- A YouTube video (with a link to your site)
- A blog posting (with a link to your site)

Appendix 8: How To Safely Update Your Wordpress Site

Wordpress updates its core system every few months. Additionally, if you are able to login to your Admin area of Wordpress, you will often see update notifications from the different plugins you have installed. Technically, you could be updating some element of Wordpress or a plugin every week.

Please understand that there is no such thing as forward compatibility with regards to your website. Anytime a new version of a plugin is released or Wordpress updates its core, you run the risk of "breaking your site" because some custom programming is not compatible with the update.

I've prepared this section to give you a walkthrough of the update process we employ internally on a quarterly basis for our clients. This process can take up to 5 hours assuming no problems appear.

- Make a backup of the source code and the database. You should be able to login to cPanel and just do a user backup. And, there are Wordpress plugins that also do a backup of your current site.
- See how your site currently works on a big screen and mobile. See how pages are rendering and check menu navigations and forms.
- You could check the Wordpress.com site and see if there are any issues they are reporting that might impact your upgrade.
- Check the plugin sites to see if they are also reporting issues.
- Run the Wordpress upgrade from your admin panel.
- Do the walkthrough again and test the pages, menus and forms.
- Then upgrade the plugins one at a time and test the site again.
- After all plugins are upgraded do a final round of testing.
- If something breaks, call your developer ☺

Appendix 9: An Expert Talks About Marketing With Videos

Excluding their potential to drive traffic to your site, videos on your website are designed for one of three purposes:

1. To serve as a first meeting
2. To demonstrate expertise
3. To sell a particular service or clarify an arcane offering

The most compelling videos have the person looking at the camera and telling us more about who he or she is than what he or she does. This could be the CEO, COO, CFO, Managing Partner, or, in the case of Bio Page Videos, an individual attorney or CPA. Ideally these are 1:00 minute videos for a Home Page, Services Page, and About Us Page. For certain industries, Testimonial Page videos with happy clients complete the job of engendering trust. Don't forget – website visitors don't get there by accident. They know what you do. Their unarticulated need is to know who you are, in the context of what you do. The result? Your first meetings will be more like second meetings, because the potential client has already decided not on your firm, but on you.

Expertise is often shown through periodic blog or newsletter videos. These can take the form of mock interviews, panel discussions, or, simply, one person speaking directly to camera. It is most cost efficient to plan out several of these – e.g. 15 pieces for weekly distribution – so they can be shot in a single day. You can have a film professional work with you to set up a mini-studio at your office and show you how to do simple edits and makeup. In that way, you can address timely issues quickly without the cost of bringing in a professional crew. The result won't be at the highest level, but, for this type of piece, will suffice.

Service providers have a particular product they'd like to push to existing clients or referral sources, such as a certain kind of trust vehicle for estate planning and asset protection purposes. In addition, some businesses – say, life insurance premium financing or R&D tax credits – require a quick clarification on their mechanisms and value propositions. These needs are best satisfied through vibrant, energetic animation. This is a longer process than live-action videos, but, generally, takes no more than a couple of months to complete.

It would be nice to be able to do any of these videos on your own or hire your nephew the film student. This is always a mistake. We all know that everyone has a very deep and personal relationship with TV and film. When something is wrong in writing, performance, makeup, framing, sound, location, music, logo animation – any number of pitfalls – the visitor will know it and immediately ascribe the discomfort in viewing it to your level of professionalism and taste. Not good.

As in anything else of importance, make sure you hire the best.

On the other hand, if all of those items are accomplished at a top level, the visitor will also recognize that, and you will immediately stand above your competition (and most others they encounter on the internet).

So make sure you hire a real professional filmmaker to do your videos and you'll get the best possible result.

Owner and Founder of Cloudwalker Videoworks, Richard Clayman uses the experience gained in 25 years as a Hollywood producer, director, writer, and executive for most major studios and networks as well as a decade teaching at top film schools such as the University of Southern California School of Cinematic Arts, to create top-quality, high-impact videos for all corporate and marketing purposes. In ten years with Cloudwalker, Richard has written, produced, and directed videos for hundreds of clients, including law firms, finance and insurance companies, non-profits, multi-million dollar corporations, and municipalities. As a "filmmaker in a sea of videographers," Richard is a seminal voice in the industry.

Link: http://www.cloudwalkerfilms.com

Appendix 10: An Expert Helps You Sell Yourself In 30 Seconds

My friend Ann Convery loves to talk about the LIZARD BRAIN.

Go Lizard! Your Business, and your Revenues, will Increase.

Which message got this CEO a $100,000 contract?

- "We produce events that create unforgettable experiences across crucial touch points: promotional marketing, sponsorship marketing and employee engagement."

- "All my clients save up to $150K in expenses, or make up to $400K in new money on every event we produce for them."

The first time this CEO used the second message at a networking event, she sat down with a $100,000 contract.

How can you access that kind of powerful effect in your business message?

Target the Lizard brain, not the thinking brain.

Why? Because the ancient, reptilian Lizard brain is the decision-maker.

The job of the thinking brain is to think. **The job of the Lizard brain is to trigger decisions.**

The reptilian, or "Lizard" part of the brain, is our survival brain, and one of its functions is to make fast decisions.

Each small decision on the part of your prospect – to listen to you, to ask for your number, to agree to a meeting – are all part of your lead generation sequence. And all of these decisions originate in the Lizard brain.

The Lizard brain's crucial function in decision-making was discovered by neuromarketers. Neuromarketing, used by companies such as Intel, eBay, and CBS, is the science-based strategy which studies the brain's responses to advertising and branding messages, and adjusts those messages to elicit even better responses.

The CEO above custom-designed her second message with critical elements for the Lizard Brain:

1. It clearly stated "What's In It for Me" to her prospects.
2. It contained stunning before-and-after results.
3. She used street language.
4. She monetized her results in a brief, compelling story.
5. She raised subtle emotions: curiosity, ambition, desire, anticipation, etc.

The rules of the Lizard brain work just as well online.

Is your website about you, or about your visitor?

Do your visitors instantly feel as if you understand them? Using Lizard brain language online can bring higher opt-ins, faster conversions, and more prospects asking to contact you.

Place the odds in your favor. Go Lizard.

Stop aiming your valuable business message at the thinking brain, which cannot make the decision to follow up.

Talk to the decision-maker, the Lizard brain, in language this brain understands.

You can be very pleasantly surprised at the results.

Anne Convery www.anneconvery.com **323-644-7955**

We've been changing business messages, and increasing revenues, for business owners and professionals for 11 years.

Appendix 11: An Expert Wealth Manager Talks About Money

To the Moon Baby. It's time to seriously grow your business.

I want you to take your business to the moon baby. Seriously. Your time is like ... Right. Now.

If I could wave some weird funky magic wand over your biz-ness, shnizz-ness, and turn it into gold - here is what I would want you to have: these 5 things. And by the way, who am I?

I'm Justin Krane. Certified Financial Planner™ professional. I manage money. But my real passion is creating money strategies for small business owners. I am a money strategy nut.

I'm wild Cray-cray. So here I go... **Numero Uno!**

We can't even get started until you master this one simple concept. Your business model. Yep.

So how do you make money? What is it that you specifically do to get paid? And how easy is it for you to do this? Do you get paid one time, or is it recurring?

I hate to pick on realtors. But they have one of the hardest business models I have seen. They work like 18 hours a day. And if that escrow doesn't close – they don't get paid. If someone doesn't qualify for a loan, realtors don't get paid. If a buyer has cold feet, the realtor doesn't get paid. I could go on and on. You get the point.

Also... Can you scale your business? Get any leverage doing it?

Scale and leverage is about getting more with less. Here are examples:

1. Instead of working with one client at a time, you could work with 4 clients at a time – in a group environment

2. Investing in some software for $100, which allows you to be
    more productive and do an additional $500 in sales

Action Plan!

Answer those questions up above in bold. Write down your answers
right here in the margin. You got this! Bottom line, you need a business
model that allows you to grow, and make profits.

Speaking of profits, that is **Numero Dos!**

Here's the deal. You can have sales. *But you need profits.*

I want your profits to be at least 10% of your sales. Or more! Example –
Sales of $5000. That means after all expenses, including what you pay
yourself – *even what you pull out of the business to live* – you need to
have a profit of 10%.

If your business can't make money, you wont make money. You will run
out of money. You also need to have a profit mindset. That means you
need to be thinking about your sales – and if you will have enough sales
to pay your business expenses.

It's about charging what you are worth. It's about not throwing money
away. Really challenging yourself to make money.

You are running an empire. Be a prosperity thinker. You can create the
financial life that you want for yourself. But you need to take action.
Don't forget about that profit mindset.

10% or more as you go to the moon!

Action plan!

What are your average sales? Multiply that # by 10%. That is what your
biz needs to make at a minimum. Write that number in the margin right
here.

Numero Tres!

Cash. Cash money.

Your business always needs to keep some cash lying around. If you have a fat stack of cash – you can say no to people.

Saying no is huge. The worst thing is when you take on projects and clients just for the money. Because you need the money.

So here is what I want you to do. I want you to have an emergency fund for your business account.

Make a list of what your fixed monthly expenses are. Keep 1-2 months of those fixed expenses in the bank. Just leave it there. It's your little security blanket.

Action Plan!

Having this amount of money in the bank will let you sleep at night. So what are your average monthly expenses? Write it in the margin of this book. Keep that amount of money in cash.

Numero Quattro! How do you even spell 4 in Spanish!?!

You need to be tracking your numbers.

But here's the deal. You don't have to do this by yourself. Just hire someone. A bookkeeper. An asst. Anyone who can help you with the numbers.

Every business needs to have a set of books. But it is really about which numbers make a difference in your business.

Start with the ones we have discussed: cash and profits. Just those 2.

Have your helper person just email you these 2 numbers every 1-2 weeks. Literally – just an email.

Knowledge is power baby. The more you know – the better decisions you will be able to make.

I got one more nugget for you on tracking. This is about your sales.

But I want to use this "losing weight analogy." You can get on the scale every day to see what you weigh. Or you can track the activities that will drive how much weight you could lose.

You could track your calories. You could track how many days a week you exercise. So why not track the stuff that will drive your sales in business? So what are the things in your business that will drive sales?

Sales conversations? The size of your email list? How many people visit your site? How much hair gel you use? Are you still reading this!!!? LOL!

So here is your **3 part Action Plan!**

- Write down the person who will to track your numbers for you.
- Write down 2 numbers you will track.
- Write down 2 things that you will track that will drive your sales.

Numero Cinco!

I love money strategy. Can you tell? But if you can dial this one thing in, and get it going real good, your biz could go to the moon...

Here I go...

You need the right message hitting the right pain point hitting the right target market.

You think that's easy? Boy. Lemme tell ya. It is a major work in progress for me. Where does the money stuff come in on this one? You are going to have to hire people to help you get this nailed down. Marketing experts, surveys, analysis, etc.

Keep this in the back of your mind as you build your business.

See you at the moon! Justin!

Justin Krane is a money strategist for small business owners. www.JKrane.com

Appendix 12: Expert Networker Reveals Easy LinkedIn Strategies

Many people can't get what they really need from LinkedIn; because of the so-so functionality, and because they don't know how to leverage it.

Let's do a reset on two levels and see if I can make it work better for you:

1. LinkedIn isn't Facebook or Twitter. No games, ego, cute thoughts, or politics. It is about getting to people who help you close deals.
2. If you are a C-level executive, and all the more so if you own a business, your LinkedIn page shouldn't read like a cheap resume.

Point 1 is straightforward. How about point 2?

What are your goals on LinkedIn?

- To establish relationships with decision-makers.
- To widen your network of intermediaries who can make referrals.

Your LinkedIn profile is the first piece of the engagement puzzle that introduces you to decision makers and intermediaries.

Don't look like a kid just out of college looking for his/her first job.

Think of your LinkedIn profile as an advertisement.

Your profile is less about what you do and more about what benefits you can offer. If your profile speaks to your value proposition, this technique is what will compel people to become interested in you, read more about you, and then view your web site to reach out and to connect with you.

The more connections you have, the more 2nd degree connections will view your profile. You need people to view your profile so they can learn more about you and your experience and what you can do for them.

My philosophy is that connections should be real. You don't need 4000 Facebook friends on LinkedIn, when you only know 350 personally.

Make each connection count, because each one can be quite valuable.

I insist on a phone call or meeting with people who connect with me. Only in this way do I know what they can do for me and what I can do for them. I then make a V-card for Outlook with all of their information, including:

- Notes on who they are;
- Notes on what they do; and,
- Even things like who we know in common.

This way, if we speak again, I will already have a frame of reference to refresh my memory, and because I can also do a word search in Outlook, when an opportunity arises, I can find these people again. People appreciate gestures like that. And if they don't want to speak, I remove them as connections.

Quality over quantity.

Don't Overlook Your LinkedIn Tagline

Here's a trick I teach my clients. Adjust the tagline in your profile below your name. Don't just write "CEO: Company X" or something similar - there's more to be done. You have a fraction of a second to get people to want to read more.

If you don't get them right away, the opportunity is gone.

- Use the tagline for more than just position and company.

- Use it for the elevator pitch as well
- Use the tagline to make you compelling.

Most people amass connections and that's where it ends. Pity.

You should be engaging them continually to remain top-of-mind.

Of course, congratulating them on work anniversaries and the like is good, but did you know that you can export your LinkedIn connections to a file and then import them into your email?

It works for Microsoft Outlook, Gmail, Yahoo! Mail, Mac OS X Address Book, and other mail programs.

There is so much more that can and should be done.

This is just the tip of the iceberg.

Good luck!

Yishai Ben Mordechai's company, Attract Leads (www.attractleads.net), uses LinkedIn to get you noticed. He drives user-specific, decision-maker traffic to your LinkedIn profile and shows you how to convert interest into a phone call or meeting where you can pitch your new prospects.

Appendix 13: Hand-to-Hand Marketing Tips by A Patent Attorney With Personality

Many Electronic Marketing is wonderful and necessary, but to call it "Social" is something of a misnomer. Real "Social Marketing" is done in person, hand-to-hand.

Yet, so many people are afraid to walk into a crowded room and try to meet people. Some have been told that the one who wins is the one who collects the most business cards while others think giving out the most business cards is more important. More about business cards later, but the truth is, that they are only a very small part of the "game" of "working a room".

There are two general kinds of settings: those in which you will get "air time" and have a chance to speak and those that are purely "mixer" in which you mix about, but there is no time for you to shine alone in front of the group.

No matter which kind of Meeting it is, you need to adapt to the size of the space, the number of people that are there (or that will be there), and you need to "take the temperature" of people there to determine how much time you can spend with each one, how much you can tell people at that time. And no matter which kind of meeting it will be, the best way to attack a room is to get there early and be one of the first people to arrive. Enter the time in your calendar for one half hour before the meeting is supposed to begin. That way you will be one of the first there, and can greet new people as they enter the room, and they will all have a chance to see you and meet you.

NETWORKING MEETING:

If you will get a chance to speak, for however long, you must carefully plan what you want people to hear from you. Do not waste time thanking the organizers, or giving preliminaries. Just "dive off the cliff" and start your talk with a line that catches people's attention and interest. Tell a story, and give visual imagery and make it memorable so that you are memorable. It is okay to pitch your services (very briefly!) after your story gets the others interested in you, but go softly. Do not forget to say your name, company, and tag line (preferably at the end of your talk, when they might care). And, if you know (or can ascertain) who else is in the room, then pitch around whomever else is there. It is not that you cannot compete, rather that you need not compete at that moment. Be respectful of others and they will appreciate it. People who do similar, but slightly different, things often become great referral partners!

Be sure to raise your hand and/or volunteer to speak if the leader is calling on people rather than going around the circle. It is your obligation to seize the floor ("Carpe Carpet") and make yourself and what you want them to hear from you relevant to the group. If you have shown up, then you need to speak up. This is not the time to be stealth and leave without being heard.

You will need to shorten (or lengthen) your presentation based on a variety of factors (be cognizant of others and do not hog the time; set your own timer), so be prepared to do so and do not slavishly rely on saying the same words each and every time. You should learn from the others in the room who have gone before you, and punch up (or tone down) your presentation accordingly.

LARGE FUNCTION (BAR, MIXER):

When you do not get a chance to address the entire group at once, you need to figure out whom and how many people to meet individually. And what to say to them. Usually, the best thing you can do is to ask them questions about themselves, their practice, their family, their hobbies. That will give you a chance to find common ground while letting them speak about their favorite subject: themselves!

It is important to figure out, to the extent you are able, which people are the best connections for you and who are the "movers and shakers" at this gathering. Now is the time to thank people for their role in organizing the event or inviting you to it. That is an excellent conversation starter, and gives you a perfectly valid reason to walk up to anyone, no matter how important or famous they may be, and say "hello" and "thank you".

It is most likely that you will know at least some people in the room already. It is your obligation to introduce the people you know to those whom you have just met (and your friends should do the same for you too). Then you must know when and how to walk away. Go to get more food, another drink, go to the bathroom, or just to say "hello" and/or "thank you" to someone else. Do not feel that it is rude to just move on; that is what is expected at these sorts of events.

Bring Your Work Colleague:

Do NOT hang out together; divide and conquer, but be able to check in with one another, introduce one another, and compare notes.

Bring Your Spouse or Associate:

This can often slow you down. It is annoying to have to introduce people and explain who everyone is. Plus, it is harder to extricate yourself when there are two of you.

The good part is that they can ask people for their name when you have forgotten, and you need a little code word or signal between you so they can know when to do that.

Set Up a Home Base Camp:

Sometimes, instead of walking around and going up to people you want to meet or say hello to, you can set up a home base camp and let other people come over to you. This really only works well if you already are well known in the organization, and people want to come over to you. The obvious downside is that you will miss saying "hello" to people who choose not to come over for whatever reason. Nonetheless, it is a powerful way of networking and gives many people a more relaxing way to attack the hordes without feeling overwhelmed.

BUSINESS CARD PRACTICES:

Giving out your business card is a great way for people to remember later who you were and how to find you again to follow up (or refer you to someone else). Just thrusting your card into someone's hand, however, is a complete and total waste of time. Some people use two pockets: one for the cards that will get entered into contacts and another pocket for those cards that will be recycled. To avoid getting out into that pocket, only give your business card if they: (1) ask for it; (2) give you theirs; or (3) seem interested in following up with you.

It is often better (more productive) to ask them for their business card, at the appropriate moment. Upon receiving a card, read both sides immediately and make a comment then and there. Discuss it with the giver. That will show that you are truly interested and will make them more interested in you. As soon as you are able to do so (and it could be right in front of them) make notes on the card to remember them and/or to follow up on what you have discussed with them.

Then, after the event is over, have your assistant enter their card and information into your contact database. Just do not add them automatically to your email distribution list and send them spam, because that will be a negative, not a positive. Use the contact information to contact them when appropriate and/or when you think of someone you would like to connect with them.

SUMMARY:

Hand-to-hand networking is a lot scarier than sending out social media blasts. Nonetheless, if you follow the tips I have given above, it can be a lot more rewarding as well. Now stop reading, and go out there and meet some people! You will thank me for it later.

Marc E. Hankin, Hankin Patent Law, APC www.HankinPatentLaw.com
(310) 979-3600. *We Protect What You Have In Mind*®

Appendix 14: The Wheel Comes Full Circle

Rebuilding: Our Digital Strategy

A few years ago, I had to go through the daunting task of rebranding my business. I had just bought out a longtime partner, who took a few employees and set up shop a few blocks away. I was nervous about having to start over with a new name and new identity when I had built a strong business development platform. My anxiety intensified a few weeks later after our marketing director told me that our search engine results were tanking. Apparently, my former partner's web guy had figured out a way to republish our firm's content under his new website in a way that made Google see us -- the authors -- as copycats. Uh oh, I thought, this is going to be a long road to get back to where we were.

Looking back, I didn't need to worry so much. Within a few months after the split, our business development was stronger than ever. We had a new name, new email address, new phone number, and business was booming. All of the gamesmanship around our web content turned out to be a whole lot of nothing. How did it come together?

It wasn't any one thing, but rather a bunch of things: a combination of old-fashioned, in-person networking and a digital strategy. I made a point of getting out for breakfasts, lunches, and networking groups to reconnect with my existing network and meet new folks. The digital strategy began with connecting with these folks and everyone else I met professionally on LinkedIn. I grew my connections to 3,000+ people. (Today, that number is approaching 7,000.)

In the past, I didn't do much to engage with the people I was connected to. My marketing activities were "siloed": I would be asked to give a presentation, would prepare a Powerpoint slide deck, deliver the talk, and move on to the next marketing activity. I might write an article for our law firm blog or give an interview to a reporter on a healthcare industry issue, but each marketing-related act would be separate and disconnected.

In the pressure to rebuild, there was too much work to do that I needed to find a way to leverage marketing time and energy more effective. It was just taking too long to create timely and interesting original content.

In order to maximize ROI, I started trying to get more leverage out of each opportunity and stretch it into not just one speech or article, but a series of bursts. In the process, I essentially created my own news cycle of publication, reuse, and circulation to extend and maximize reach.

- For example, when I was asked to give a talk on addiction treatment billing fraud, in addition to putting together a slide deck, I wrote up a short "teaser" article and a longer article based on the same content.
- Rather than rely on the organization hosting the event, I would post a lead-up article about the talk on our website in the week or two before. I would share the fact that the event was coming up as an activity update on LinkedIn, Twitter, and Google+, and then share the teaser article.
- I would post activity updates on the day of the talk with photos, and then a link to the longer form article posted on our blog. If the article had good substance, I would wait a few days to see how much circulation the activity update received and then publish it on Pulse.
- Sometimes, I would also publish my slide deck on Slideshare. As a result, what would have once been a single event – a talk – heard by 50 people who heard it live turned into a multi-week news cycle that touched over 1,000 people. I knew this strategy was working from the comments and informal feedback from people who hadn't been there.

I realized that, while a small group of people cared about the details of my message, a bigger cohort would be just happy to know that this was a matter of subject matter expertise.

While the feedback that people were seeing our content was one level of success, the even bigger payoff came when we struck a nerve with content that was timely on an issue that other people were worrying about. Several times, we would publish something that went viral, with others reposting our content on Facebook and elsewhere, generating thousands of views. We haven't yet figured out a model to hit that level consistently, but the few times it has happened, we have caught a powerful "wave".

Over the past several years, the strategy has continued to evolve. I established a personal blog to share things I was thinking about beyond the confines of legal issues. I built a Twitter following. We learned to use press releases, to build good relationships with journalists, do webinars, and host many more of our own events. We continue to explore new tactics (Facebook, Instagram, etc.) and figure out what's working and what needs work. We may have a long way to go to reach the level of online visibility and brand engagement of big consumer companies, but in our little niche, we seem to be ahead of the pack in strengthening our attachments with our clients, referral sources, and others in the industries we serv. At the end of the day, building business comes down to showing expertise and remaining visible across a strong network.

Harry Nelson founded Nelson Hardiman, a boutique healthcare law firm, in 2004. He is an attorney who advises clients on healthcare regulatory compliance and business strategy. His vision of the future of the healthcare industry has driven next-generation healthcare ideas and initiatives to realization. Harry also has over two decades of experience with crisis response and organizational "turn-around" problem-solving on industry challenges, with a focus on digital health, behavioral health, and the transition to value-based care. He co-chairs the investment committee of a healthcare investment fund, Adaptive Healthcare, and sits on the boards of several non-profit and for-profit healthcare organizations. Harry lives and works in Los Angeles, California.

Introducing the Inevitable

SHAMELESS PLUG

REFER A CLIENT. GET PAID!

- Website Design
- Wordpress Website
- Ecommerce Store
- Search Engine Optimization
- Pay-Per-Click Advertising
- Facebook Advertising
- Social Media Marketing

GET 15% REFERRAL FEES

http://www.GetVisible.com/referrals

Made in the USA
San Bernardino, CA
10 October 2016